# The Best of the

# Monday Morning Marketing

# Memo

By

## Steven Howard

# The Best of the Monday Morning Marketing Memo

For reprint permission, please contact:
> Steven Howard
> c/o Caliente Press
> 1775 E Palm Canyon Drive, Suite 110-198
> Palm Springs, CA   92264
> U.S.A
> Email: steven@howard-marketing.com

Published by:
> Caliente Press
> 1775 E Palm Canyon Drive, Suite 110-198
> Palm Springs, CA 92264
> U.S.A.
> Email: CalientePress@verizon.net

Cover Design:  Lee Chee Yih

# Dedication

*This book is dedicated to*

*Melvin Tan Chek Shang*

*Once a protégé, now an outstanding marketer in his own right.*

*Once my student, now my advisor.*

*And always a valued friend.*

The following phrases used in this book are trademarked by the author:

*If it touches the customer, it's a marketing issue.*™

*The art of keeping good customers.*™

*Customer Retention: The Art of Keeping Good Customers*™

*The Art of Keeping Good Customers.*™

# Table of Contents

## Tools

# Introduction

For many years the *Monday Morning Marketing Memo* was one of the most popular marketing e-newsletters. At its peak it had a global readership of over 5600, comprising mostly business owners, entrepreneurs, senior executives, and marketing practitioners in organizations big and small.

Written and distributed (almost) weekly to subscribers, the key topics of the *Monday Morning Marketing Memo* were: advertising, branding, corporate image management, customer loyalty, customer retention marketing, research, marketing strategies, responsibility, sales management skills, search engine optimization, and topical marketing issues of the day.

## The Best of the Monday Morning Marketing Memo

These weekly thought starters were written with my core marketing philosophy — *it if touches the customer, it's a marketing issue*™ — in mind.

Slightly edited, revised and updated as necessary, the 42 *Monday Morning Marketing Memos* compiled here are the ones that generated the most commentary, queries, and feedback from readers around the world.

While the electronic newsletter version of the *Monday Morning Marketing Memo* no longer exists, the *Monday Morning Marketing Memo* has been reborn as a weekly blog at www.TheMondayMorningMarketingMemo.com.

Like its previous version, the *Monday Morning Marketing Memo Blog* is written to help business executives, entrepreneurs, and marketers focus on the key marketing topics that will help you grow your businesses, retain customers, and leverage your corporate brands.

# The Best of the Monday Morning Marketing Memo

*The Best of the Monday Morning Marketing Memo* were chosen from the nearly 250 weekly memos I penned over a six-year period. I hope you find them as enjoyable and useful as our initial readers did.

As an extra bonus, we have added at the end of the book five of the tools and checklists provided to our clients and *Monday Morning Marketing Memo* readers over the years.

Best wishes for continued success.

Steven Howard
June 2015

**#16**

# The Value of a Good Corporate Brand

Let's focus our attention on the subject of corporate image.

While I was conducting research for my first book, *Corporate Image Management: A Marketing Discipline For the 21st Century*, I began looking for illustrations to prove the value of a strong corporate image.

I knew intuitively that a strong corporate image would provide several levels of value to an organization — such as financial value, market place value, human resource value and, of course, customer value.

But how to prove this?

Well, an example from the automotive world probably best illustrates the market value of a powerful corporate brand.

In the late 1980s, Toyota and General Motors created a joint venture company in Freemont, California called New United Motor Manufacturing Inc. (NUMMI).

The NUMMI plant produced two identical cars: the Toyota Corolla and the General Motors Geo Prizm. These two cars were produced on the same manufacturing line, using the same raw materials, the same labor, and the same manufacturing process; basically the same of everything. In the computer world we would call these two car models "pin for pin compatible."

The only difference between the two models was that some of them carried the Toyota Corolla brand name and some of them had the General Motors GM Prizm marque.

## The Best of the Monday Morning Marketing Memo

Being identical in all but brand name, they should sell for approximately the same price and depreciate at about the same rate, correct?

Perhaps so, but they didn't.

The Toyota Corolla sold in 1989 for about 10% more than the GM Geo Prizm. It then depreciated more slowly than the Geo Prizm, resulting in a second-hand value almost 18% higher than the American-branded model after five years.

Why the differences?

One has to conclude that the relative strength of the Toyota brand and corporate name, over the General Motors name in the late 1980s and early 1990s, played the first significant role. If car buyers perceived a Toyota named car to be superior to a GM car in the same model class, they would be willing to pay a higher sticker price.

But that wasn't the entire difference, according to a study by the Boston Consulting Group. The BCG study reported that the after-sales service provided by the Toyota dealer network sustained, and even boosted, the perceived edge of the Toyota name.

In other words, the corporate image management process taken by Toyota to ensure that the service departments at its dealer network wouldn't tarnish or deteriorate the Toyota brand helped to reinforce the positive attributes of the Toyota identity.

These positive attributes had already given it an edge in the marketplace vis-a-vis a direct competitor brand manufactured in the same facility, using the same materials and labor.

This example shows the direct value of a powerful and well-managed corporate brand.

It was stories such as this, as I continued to conduct my research into the value of corporate branding and corporate image, that led me to conclude that corporate image management is one of the most powerful and potent marketing and management tools available to senior executives for the 21st century.

**KEY POINT**: corporate image management is one of the most powerful marketing and management tools available.

**TAKING ACTION**: what are your internal processes for managing your corporate brand and corporate image?

What is the weakest link in your corporate image management chain? What steps can be taken immediately to strengthen this weakest link?

What is the strongest aspect of your corporate image? How can this be further leveraged to develop market leadership for your products or services?

**#30**

# Corporate Image Management

The corporate image is a dynamic and profound affirmation of the nature, culture and structure of an organization. This applies equally to corporations, businesses, government entities, and non-profit organizations.

Looked at from a marketing perspective, corporate brand management needs to be an on-going, synergistic management tool, not the one-time "corporate image exercise" as practiced by so many organizations and almost all corporate identity consultants.

The corporate brand provides a mechanism for the organization to:

- Differentiate itself from competition.

- Create recognized added-value to the products and services marketed or delivered by the organization.

- Attract and maintain customer relationships in order to prosper in an increasingly competitive and constantly changing global marketplace.

The corporate image also represents the highest level of brand personality and characteristics that can be created and communicated to customers and marketing partners [and hence the linkage to relationship marketing].

In today's world of deteriorating product brand power, rising perceptions of parity products, reducing employee loyalty, and increasing competition, the corporate brand image has taken on renewed importance.

Previously, a company's visual identity system was sufficient to project and protect the image of the organization. Today, all aspects of the corporate brand image need to be managed, from the refinement of the mission statement to how well the troops on the front line understand, communicate, and portray this mission.

Corporate image management matches the expectations and understanding of both customers and employees about what the organization stands for, where it is heading, and what its core strengths, traditions, and principles are.

The underlining principle of this discipline is simply this: *if it touches the customer, it's a marketing issue.*™

Nothing touches the customer more than how he or she perceives your corporate image. This fundamental perception will be a major factor that determines whether the customer will decide to conduct business with you and, more important, enter into a long-term and mutually rewarding relationship with your organization.

There may be no greater marketing issue than management of the corporate image in today's increasingly competitive markets.

Without a doubt, corporate image management will be a key marketing discipline well into the 21st century.

The ultimate battleground for winning and maintaining customer relationships now takes place in the minds, hearts, emotions, and perceptions of your customers.

**KEY POINT**: the corporate image represents the highest level of brand personality that can be created and communicated to customers and marketing partners.

**TAKING ACTION**: where and how can you place greater resources in winning the battle for the minds, hearts, emotions, and perceptions of customers?

Is your corporate brand giving you sufficient differentiation in the market? Why or why not?

How can your corporate brand provide added value to the products and services marketed and delivered by your organization?

What does your organization stand for? Where is it headed? What are its most important core strengths, traditions, and principles? Are these found within your corporate image, as perceived by your key constituents?

**#46**

# The Sales / Service Relationship

Many organizations like to segment their customer service function from their sales activities. I believe this is a mistake.

The closer you can entwine your service and sales activities, the more successful you are likely to be. After all, the customer rarely segments a sales activity from a service activity. To him or her, all your activities are service interrelated!

The formula for weaving these two activities together is to:

1) turn service opportunities into sales opportunities, and

2) follow up on sales opportunities to provide efficient and appreciated service.

Another way of expressing this is: SALES = SERVICE = SUCCESS.

Some people like to argue that this expression should read "sales + service = success." But that is where I disagree. That is the way of doing things today, with sales being one activity and service being another, with little or no integration.

Changing your mindset to SALES = SERVICE = SUCCESS means you understand that success comes when there is no segmentation between selling and service.

In today's age of consultative selling, one of the best services your organization can provide is to sell a customer the right product at the right time that provides the right solution for his or her particular need.

Now that's a true service. One that every customer is likely to appreciate.

People often ask me, "How do you know if a customer is satisfied?"

The simple, and best, answer is: ask.

Be proactive. Call and ask the customer:

*"Did everything go as expected?"*

*"Have we delivered as promised?"*

*"Have we met your expectations?"*

Staff should be encouraged to never be afraid of having to deal with problems. What if you do call up and there is a problem? Well, at least you are now aware of it, and you have an opportunity to fix the immediate problem — before it grows into something larger and unmanageable. And by doing so, you not only show the customer that you care about them, but that you are also willing to make sure that they are completely satisfied — two concerns of customers that they will value highly.

Also, not following up always results in a missed selling opportunity.

After all, when is the best time to start the next sales cycle?

Anytime the customer is satisfied with you.

So, if nothing has gone wrong and the customer is fully satisfied, that is the ideal time to start working toward the next repeat order. Or, once you have corrected any problems and have achieved customer satisfaction through your servicing efforts, you are in an ideal position to start working towards the next sale.

The Golden Rule of selling: keep the customer satisfied, not just sold.

Remember the 3-step equation from an earlier *Monday Morning Marketing Memo*:

1) Quality results in customer satisfaction.

2) Customer satisfaction results in repeat buys.

3) Repeat purchases lead to customer loyalty.

By weaving together your sales and service mindsets, and being proactive in your customer care efforts, you will achieve the customer loyalty levels you are seeking.

Marketing is not rocket science. In fact, marketing success really boils down to two key principles: understanding customer needs and delivering upon the promises the organization makes. You can achieve these two principles through a full understanding of the sales/service relationship.

**KEY POINT**: it is important to weave together your sales and service activities so that they appear seamless to the customer.

**TAKING ACTION**: are you sales people capable of superior service? Are your service people capable of superior selling? How can you fix any gaps that exist?

How can you make your staff more proactive in their customer care activities?

How can you inculcate the mantra SALES = SERVICE = SUCCESS throughout your organization?

What steps can you implement to keep your VIP customers satisfied, not just sold?

# Succeeding in Sales

Not everyone is cut out for a career, or even an assignment in sales.

Additionally, it is often difficult for people to make the switch from "Customer Service Officer," a role with an emphasis on serving the customer, to that of "Customer Sales Representative" and a need to be a professional sales person.

However, in today's world, where customers have numerous choices of service and product providers, an organization without a sales culture featuring a core of well-trained, highly motivated sales professionals, is not going to be as successful as it would with these two ingredients.

Selling is a people business. So what does it take to be successful in selling?

A partial, and admittedly by no means complete, list of personal criteria for succeeding in selling includes:

1. **Customer Focus and Concern** — a successful sales person will build relationships based on trust, honesty, integrity, and concern for his customers. They have to be able to understand, from your customer's perspective, the needs, wants, and desires of each individual customer. What are your customers' key needs, wants, and desires and how can your organization satisfy these cost efficiently, or through adding value, or both?

2. **Loyalty to the Needs of the Customer** — having the ability to be an internal advocate and fighter for the customer, and being able to lead

(directly or indirectly) internal teams and processes toward the absolute satisfaction of your customers.

3. **Accepting and Learning from Rejection –** everyone in sales experiences rejection. A sales person cannot take rejection personally, but must use each instance as a learning experience. Those who allow sales rejections to upset them personally and emotionally are likely to carry these emotions into their personal lives. An unhappy or emotionally distraught person is unlikely to find success in a sales career.

4. **Understanding the Value of Selling –** customers today cannot be expected to know all there is about your products. When they need more information, they turn to your sales forces to help educate them. This is why consultative

selling approaches, rather than the old fashioned hard sell approaches, are working best in so many industries. Selling is a value-added process, when it is done right. Each sales person needs to be a critical component in this value adding job function.

5. **Being a Constant Student** — successful sales people are not born, they are well trained and tend to be constant learners. A desire to constantly upgrade one's skills is a key criteria for success, resulting in a self-propelled drive to read, listen to audio recordings, or watch DVDs, from successful sales people and others about factors that impact their selling skills and personal self motivation.

6. **Believing in themselves, your products and your services** — customers can easily tell

when a sales person does not fully believe in the products and services they are selling. Success requires a complete belief in what you are selling, including full confidence and belief in one's own consultative selling ability.

7.  **Commitment** — at a minimum, a three-level commitment is required:

    a)  A commitment to continuing trying, no matter what the odds or what one's recent experiences have been.

    b)  A commitment to focus on the needs of the customer, not only on the needs of one's own organization.

    c)  A commitment to one's self to constantly upgrade skills and to constantly monitor one's own motivation requirements.

8.  **Goal Setter** — the old adage that "what gets measured gets accomplished" is very true in sales. A successful sales person will set his/her

own stretch goals, ones that focus on the selling process (number of attempts/calls, hours spent upgrading skills, etc.) as well as on outcomes (sales, success ratios, etc.).

9. **Honesty and Trustworthiness** — one cannot build a long-term career in sales without being fully honest and trusted. As in point number one above, client relationships must be built on honesty, integrity, trust, and a true concern for one's customers. After all, customers prefer to purchase from those they can trust.

10. **Keeping Outgoing Personality Under Control** — many people think they will be good at selling because they have an outgoing personality and they enjoy interacting with people. While it is true that an extrovert has many tendencies and qualities of a good sales

person, it is also important to remember that one of the most critical selling skills is that of listening. An outgoing personality that asks interesting questions is far more likely to be successful in sales than a person who only likes to talk about themselves and/or their products and services.

11. **Enthusiasm** — last, but certainly not least, is to have positive enthusiasm for one's job, products, company, and even life in general. Positive and enthusiastic people are so much more pleasant to deal with that we all find ourselves buying from them just because the sales/buying experience has been so enjoyable.

There are many more personal criteria required for being successful in sales, but this list is a good start. And without these 11 criteria as one's core personal competencies, all other personal attributes will not lead to the kind of success one is capable of achieving.

**KEY POINT**: successful sales people are well trained and are constantly learning how to upgrade their skills.

**TAKING ACTION**: what can you do on a regular basis to upgrade your selling skills?

Are you setting sales goals strictly on final outcomes (i.e. sales targets) or do you also set goals for each step of the sales process?

Do you have a regular process for reviewing rejection, so that each sales rejection becomes a learning experience?

Where can the selling process (which is the buying process from the customer's perspective) add value to the customer? Are you placing enough emphasis and resources in this area?

**#52**

# Tell Me More

When you ask a customer, or a client, a question, there is a great tendency to take the customer's response at face value, making the assumption that the answer given is a full and complete answer.

Many times this simply is not so.

Customer responses are a bit like swimming suits. What they reveal is most interesting. What they keep covered, however, is vital.

Few customers are going to tell you everything about how they feel and think, or everything about their needs, wants, and desires.

# The Best of the Monday Morning Marketing Memo

It is up to the inquiring professional sales person to dig deeper into customer responses through probing and follow-up questioning.

Good sales people are like journalists chasing a good story. You do not just want the facts. You want to know the who, what, and why behind the story (in this case, the customer's response).

Sales people need to be taught the same basic requirements as journalists: do not come back until you have discovered the 5 Ws and 1 H. This is the who, what, where, when, why, and how that gives you the story behind the story, or the deeper answers behind the stated responses.

Or, to use another analogy from my favorite pastime (scuba diving), you cannot understand the whole structure of a coral reef by only snorkeling around the top of the reef. To really see the beauty of the reef, and its full composition, it is usually necessary to dive a bit deeper.

The same is true with customer situations. In order to ensure you fully understand the customer's situation, and all of the factors impacting that situation, you need to dive a little deeper through your questioning tactics.

Of course, one does not want to be seen as an inquisitor, or as a busy body, when having a discussion with a customer.

That is why the direct approach to question asking often does not work very well.

Instead, try the indirect route. My favorite way of asking a follow up question to a customer is the simple phrase, "*tell me more.*"

This not only signals to the customer that I am listening, but that I am interested in what they have to say.

Being interested in what the customer has to say, of course, is an extremely valuable way of building credibility, trust, and confidence with a customer or prospect. After all, it is human nature to want to be listened to.

Speaking of listening, I often tell sales people to remember that "God gave us two ears and one mouth, and we should use these in that proportion." In other words, a good sales person will listen twice as often as he or she talks when engaged in a discussion with a customer.

Sales people have a great tendency to jump into the conversation, and often rush to present solutions and ideas before the real needs of the customer have surfaced in the conversation. This is a common mistake and often results in the customer walking away saying that they are not ready to buy yet (when what they really mean is that they haven't found someone who has listened thoroughly enough to understand their problem or situation).

It takes a great deal of discipline to hold off from presenting solutions you believe are viable for the customer and to continue probing. But this discipline will lead to better understanding of customer needs, and higher successful closing rates.

Three simple words: tell me more.

That is all it takes to be a good journalist, or a good sales person.

Good luck, and good selling.

**KEY POINT**: being interested in what the customer has to say, by asking good follow up questions, is an extremely valuable way of building credibility, trust, and confidence with a customer or prospect.

**TAKING ACTION**: what other phrases can you use to get customers to tell you more about their wants, needs, and desires?

Evaluate the probing skills of your sales staff. Where are the areas for the most improvement? Who is in the best position to coach them on probing skills?

# Nobody Noticed

A week ago yesterday I flew from Melbourne to Singapore. Just another day, another international journey.

Except that it was not just another day. It was my birthday. And nobody noticed!

As a result, the airline and the hotel that I encountered that day missed a huge opportunity to provide this customer with an extraordinary experience.

Instead, I only received their "ordinary good, everyday customer experience." And yet, there was really no excuse for this.

While checking in for my flight, the customer service person at the counter used my passport details to create the

"Express Lane" immigration card that they give out to all Business and First Class customers. That card has my birth date details.

This airline is one of my two favorites, and I have already attained Platinum Level status in their frequent flyer program, because of my loyalty and the number of long-haul trips I have made this year between Australia and Asia. Their main competitor on the Australia to Asia sector sent me a birthday card that arrived two days before this journey. But as far as I know, I haven't received a thing from this particular carrier.

Upon arrival in Singapore I proceed to the well-established, five-star Asian hotel chain where the three-day workshop I was conducting was being held. This time the lady at the check-in counter took my passport and completed the various boxes on the hotel's registration card. I noticed that she properly recorded both my passport details and my date of birth. Again, there was no correlation to entry of the data and the fact that it coincided with that particular date.

In reflecting upon this, I see that the hotel staff has been well trained to fill in forms quickly and efficiently. But they take no notice of the information that is being recorded. I am just another customer to be moved as quickly as possible from the check-in desk to the hotel room.

Now I did not expect birthday cakes and birthday songs from either of these organizations.

I did think, however, that they would have had systems in place so that a personal greeting would have been proffered. On the airline, the Chief Cabin Officer always walks around, introduces himself/herself, and personally welcomes aboard their FFP customers. And while this did take place during the flight, I would have been extremely pleased had he quietly said, "Oh, Mr. Howard, I see that today is your birthday. Happy Birthday from all of us at XYZ Airlines." Instead, he only checked to see if I needed an immigration form for arrival into Singapore.

The same goes for the hotel. Why don't they have a system in place for the General Manager or the Resident Manager to send a short birthday note to the rooms of the guests who are traveling away from home on their special day? I am not suggesting that they need to send flowers or a bottle of wine, but just a personal note (or even better a phone call) would go a long way in telling the guest that they are not just another customer in residence on a typical day.

There was nothing to fault in the normal service delivered by either of these two service providers. Both were efficient, friendly, and up to standard.

On any other day, the service delivery would have been proper and sufficient.

But this was not any other day. It was my birthday.

And hence the opportunity for an extra-ordinary customer experience was missed. By both.

**KEY POINT**: a customer's birthday is a great opportunity to provide an extra-ordinary level of personal attention and/or service.

**TAKING ACTION**: are you capturing data about customers that could be put to better use?

Are your people real good at completing forms, yet taking no notice of the information being collected? How can you put to better use the information on customers you collect?

What important events in your customers' lives are you overlooking?

How can you make a special day in your customer's life even more special?

**#96**

# 7 Cs of Customer Retention

Many companies around the world are recognized by consumers for worldwide excellent service. Companies such as McDonald's, Singapore Airlines, Federal Express, L.L. Bean, and Citibank are successful because they know exactly what their customers expect and then they satisfy these customer expectations (most of the time).

At McDonald's, every employee — in every country around the world — knows the company stands for quality, service, cleanliness, and value. Every McDonald's employee also knows exactly what each of these elements means in terms of HOW to do business with McDonald's customers.

At Citibank, the service quality goal is to set and consistently meet service performance standards that satisfy the customer and profit the bank. In other words, at Citibank the customer is the final judge of service and the bank invests an inordinate amount of money each year in tracking its customer satisfaction levels.

While all customers are unique, and use different values to make purchasing decisions, there are seven common customer expectations for customer service that have basically become the MINIMUM LEVEL that today's customers DEMAND be met by all the organizations from which they buy. Because these are the minimum requirements, they are also the ones that must be met if you are to achieve any significant level of customer retention.

The 7 Cs of Customer Retention are:

**Caring Attitude** — employees that are caring, friendly, helpful, care/show empathy, value me as a customer, apologizes for company errors.

**Customized Practices** — flexibility in applying most, if not all, company policies, simple documentation, forms that are easy to understand and use, suspension of disputed charges, willingness to extend additional services, ability of the organization at all key contact points to know and understand the customer's relationship with us.

**Competent CCPs** — having customer contact personnel who communicate well and accurately, take action, meet commitments, keep customers constantly informed of a situation's status, and who are fully aware of all the organization's products, services, procedures, and policies.

**Call/Visit Once** — the customer's initial contact person in your organization handles the problem, or gets it resolved. The CCP or contact person makes necessary decisions and the customer only needs to explain the problem once (even if moved to another service provider). All contacts know the customer's account status, as well as the nature of the problem under resolution.

**Convenient Access** — your operating hours of stores, branches, outlets, offices, and call centers are structured with the needs of customers in mind. Your access numbers are easy to get through, are answered promptly, and the length of time on hold and the number of transfers internally before the problem is resolved are kept to a minimum. Your website is easy to understand, navigate, use and the ordering process is simple and caters for international orders (if you are willing to ship goods and products outside your home country).

**Compressed Cycle Times** — customers receive an immediate response to enquiries, products and services meet customers' timing, adjustments or changes (such as address changes) are made before the next billing or statement cycle, and your organization provides consistently quick turnaround (especially for problem solving).

**Committed Follow Through** — the CCP and/or customer's contact person commits to what/when/how, follows-up to confirm action, checks on satisfaction level, and your organization takes corrective action to prevent reoccurrence of an error or problem.

These 7 Cs are the minimum requirements your customers have. And if you do not deliver well against these criteria, then you cannot expect to have high levels of customer satisfaction, customer loyalty, or customer retention.

Last week we gave you a checklist of items that you can use in monitoring your business unit's service delivery on these seven customer expectations. As several other successful, customer-focused organizations have done, please put this checklist to good use and you will be well on your way to achieving high levels of customer retention, or what I like to call *the art of keeping good customers.*™

**KEY POINT:** there are seven common customer expectations for customer service that have basically become the MINIMUM LEVEL that today's customers DEMAND be met by the organizations from which they buy from.

**TAKING ACTION:** do all your customer contact personnel have caring, friendly attitudes? Do they exhibit empathy towards customers at all times? How could this be improved?

How flexible are your company policies? Could they be made more flexible? Would greater flexibility be appreciated by your customers?

How simple and easy-to-use is your documentation? How can this be made more simple or easier to use?

When was the last time you asked your customers these same questions?

**#99**

# Customer Service Creed

The importance of focusing on customer needs, wants, and desires is a key theme in every seminar and keynote speech I give.

I have long advocated that too many businesses are being run in the pursuit of short-term shareholder value (i.e. share price) and not in the pursuit of long-term shareholder value through solving customer problems profitably and from developing long-term customer loyalty.

Now that a significant portion of the global economy is undergoing a slow (or negative) growth phase, the solitary pursuit by senior executives in trying to constantly push the share price higher and higher is coming home to scorch them.

**The way to create long-term shareholder value is to create and keep customers.**

In order to develop strong customer retention strategies, you need to have an organization-wide customer service creed in place.

Here's a generic Customer Service Creed that you might be able to adapt for your own purposes:

1.  Every employee has customers, either internal or external (or both). Everyone in the organization must *walk the talk* during every customer point of interaction.

2.  Treat all employees as special, just as you would treat all customers as special. How you treat your staff is mirrored in the way they treat your customers.

3. Empower employees who are engaged in regular contact with external customers to make decisions. Establish relaxed levels of authority and alternate chain of commands. Not all decisions should, or need to, come to managers. Trust your staff, having given them appropriate guidelines to work within.

4. Customer service does not end when the customer has paid for the product and taken it home. Customer service must continue after the sale, just as it must come before the sale.

5. Allow the customer to talk. Look at them. Be interested in them. Summarize what they are saying. Treat each customer as a unique individual with individual needs, wants, and desires and never as someone who is making the same request you have heard before.

6.  To the customer, each individual they interact with is the organization. Eliminate the "we/they" thinking. Success comes when you think of the word *"us"* when dealing with customers.

7.  It is much easier to create a positive impression than to erase or correct a negative one.

8.  Let the customer win. Then you both win.

9.  Your competition is anyone the customer compares you with.

10. Reward, recognize, and celebrate your customer service successes. This creates momentum for future success stories.

To win today's marketing battles, you might want to consider creating and publicizing, both internally and externally, your own Customer Service Creed.

And remember, when the customer wins, you also win!

**KEY POINT #1**: in order to develop strong customer retention strategies, you need to have an organization-wide customer service creed in place.

**KEY POINT #2**: when the customer wins, you also win!

**TAKING ACTION**: do you treat employees as special? Is how your organization treats its own staff reflected in the ways your staff treat customers?

What impressions of your organization do your customers take away with them after each and EVERY interaction with your organization?

How can you eliminate the "we/they" thinking between your staff and your customers?

**#100**

# Creating a Culture of Service Professionalism

How is a service-successful organization different? To start with, such organizations build employee professionalism in several ways.

They establish the personal accountability of individual employees. They create service teams. They open multiple communication channels with their staff and use these rigorously.

They accomplish employee professionalism by rewarding extraordinary service actions and informing staff how their jobs fit into the entire organization. They explain to staff the importance of customer service, the need for problem-free service, and the benefits to the organization of delivering excellent service to customers.

None of these tactics is necessarily revolutionary. What's most outstanding is how energetically and comprehensively excellent companies work at their total programs. The strategies and tactics for excellent customer service are ingrained at all levels of the organization, not just within a handful of specific departments or outlets.

Underlying all these imperatives is a simple belief: **customer relations mirror employee relations.**

Employees must first perceive and experience within their own organizations whatever it is that management wants customers to perceive and experience. This operates most directly with customer contact employees, the pivotal people in any service business. They internalize messages passed within their organizations and in turn broadcast these messages to customers.

A recent study of bank branch employees and their customers confirmed this relationship. When employees reported that their branch emphasized service, customers reported superior banking experiences, and were more highly satisfied.

Some proven techniques for achieving a culture of service professionalism include:

a) Use of staff attitudes (people surveys) as a diagnostic tool for understanding staff views on service and service delivery. Action plans undertaken to address staff issues and concerns should be part of the business unit's overall service delivery strategy.

b) Use of service recognition programs that result in winners serving as role models for fellow staff members. Also, service awards for the office or business unit are based on service indicator performance.

c) Internal performance improvement teams are established within offices and business units to work on improving service delivery. Participating staff learn new skills and are motivated to perform at even higher levels.

Like marketing itself, creating a culture of service professionalism is not rocket science. But it does take effort, leadership, dedication, and continued communications to make it happen.

It also means having a management team that is not solely focused on achieving "the most efficient processes."

This is because many aspects of excellent customer service delivery require personal, customized handling.

A good example is the "telephone hell" that many customers have to go through to speak to someone. All these automated voice response systems are fine (you know, "press 1 if you have product A, press 2 if you have product B, etc.) and highly efficient *from the organization's perspective*.

But *from the customer's perspective* these systems are annoying, dehumanizing, and denigrate the customer service image of the organization being contacted.

A taxi company I used to use in Singapore had it right. Their automated incoming call system had just two options: press 1 if you wanted a taxi immediately, or press 2 if you wanted to book a cab for a later time. If you pressed 1, and you were a regular customer calling from your normal phone, the taxi was sent immediately to pick you up and the system provided an estimated time of arrival. If you pressed 2, a customer service person came on line, took your details, and arranged for the taxi to collect you at your requested time and place.

Simple, short, and sweet – while both highly efficient *and* highly personalized.

The bottom line for creating a culture of service professionalism is twofold:

a) Treat your employees positively and they will treat your customers positively.

b) High-tech is great from the perspective of organizational efficiency, but high-touch is even better from the perspective of your customers.

When you accomplish both of these, you will achieve a great bond with both your customers and your staff.

**KEY POINT #1:** customer relations mirror employee relations.

**KEY POINT #2:** high-tech is great and efficient, but high-touch is what keeps your customers coming back.

**TAKING ACTION:** Do you treat employees as special? Is the way your organization treats its own staff reflected in the way your staff treat customers?

What impressions of your organization do your customers have after each and *every* interaction with your organization?

How can you eliminate the "us and them" thinking between your staff and your customers?

How do you reward, recognize, and celebrate your customer service success stories? How can these be ingrained in the culture and practices of your entire organization?

How can you use technology to make your customer experiences simple, short, and sweet?

**#101**

# Service Excellence Attributes

There are several attributes regularly displayed by staff who consistently perform at high levels of customer service delivery. These attributes are the ones that differentiate Service Excellence winners from other staff. They are also the attributes that managers will want to search for in future hiring and staff transfer decisions.

These attributes are:

**Cares for the customer** — Service Excellence winners are sensitive to customers' needs and are frequently described as customer advocates. They display a sincere willingness to listen to customers and to assist wherever and whenever they can.

**Displays Consistent Service Ethic** — Service Excellence winners are committed to doing the best job possible every day. They assume ownership of problems in spite of adverse circumstances or conditions. They work well under pressure and adapt quickly to new assignments.

**Exceed Production/Quality Goals** — Service Excellence winners regularly exceed their volume, timeliness, accuracy, and quality goals.

**Solves Problems Creatively** — Service Excellence winners proactively seek alternative methods to improve procedures, reduce costs, and improve quality. They place customers' needs above internal concerns.

**Works Well With Co-workers** — Service Excellence winners have excellent working relationships with co-workers. They are always willing to help others and to share knowledge freely.

**Helps in Other Areas** — Service Excellence winners display a desire to learn jobs outside their immediate areas of responsibility. They frequently volunteer to assist on task forces and special assignments, notwithstanding the longer hours required.

**Exhibits High Energy and Enthusiasm** — Service Excellence winners exhibit positive attitudes that impact morale within their units. They have the ability to motivate those around them to work harder and smarter on behalf of customers.

Can you teach the above skills? You can, in the same way that you can teach ethics, good manners, proper social behavior, and fellowship to mankind. For in effect, what really differentiates a service excellence deliverer from anyone else is how they interact with their customers, both external and internal. It is really a personal attribute, sort of like being a good citizen or being a good neighbor.

In addition to teaching the above skills, it would be best to create the right internal corporate culture where these skills and attributes can flourish. As we discussed the *Monday Morning Marketing Memo* on *Creating A Culture of Service Professionalism,* none of the tactics employed by service excellent companies to build employee professionalism are necessarily revolutionary. Most important, however, these tactics are energetically and comprehensively inculcated throughout service excellence organizations on an on-going, never-ending basis.

Over the past few weeks we have discussed the Five Dimensions of Service Quality Excellence, the 7 Cs of Customer Retention, crafting a Customer Service Creed,

Creating A Culture of Service Professionalism, and the key attributes of service excellence providers.

The path to becoming a Service Excellence Company is figuring out how to integrate these concepts into your own comprehensive, energetic, interactive, on-going, and never-ending program.

For, at the end of the day, excellent customer service drives customer satisfaction; resulting in a strategic advantage for your organization with a direct impact on repeat business, customer recommendations to others, market share, revenue, and profit.

If your business focus is on customer satisfaction, all these other items on your corporate scorecard will fall naturally into place.

**KEY POINT**:  the attributes regularly displayed by staff who consistently perform at high levels of customer service delivery are different from other staff.

**TAKING ACTION**:  how do you recognize and reward staff who assume ownership of problems in spite of adverse circumstances or conditions?

How do you reward, recognize and celebrate your customer service success stories?  How can these be ingrained in the culture and practices of your entire organization?

Do your training programs focus only on functional skills, or do they also incorporate activities that help to grow personal attributes, social skills, and interpersonal communications skills?

Is your organization or business unit a high energy one or a de-motivating, energy-sapping one?

**#122**

# Think Customers

How do you call or refer to the people who buy your goods and services? What descriptive names do you use? What terminology do you use to discuss them?

Your pronoun of choice may include passengers, guests, participants, clients, patients, and a whole host of other words.

However, there is only word that should be used — customers.

Here is how the choice of descriptive can alter the way you and your colleagues think about your customers:

Passengers sit in airplane seats eating boring meals and attempting to be entertained by movies on small screens.

**Customers are flyers with individual** needs, wants, and desires whose travel experiences begin from the time the journey is planned to the time they collect their luggage at their final destination.

Δ Δ Δ Δ Δ

Cargo shippers hand over freight that is then stored and transported in the belly of a plane or the hold of a ship.

**Customers are the people** shipping or receiving the precious (to them) cargo being carried and transported.

Δ Δ Δ Δ Δ

Hotel guests check in, check out, occasionally dine in house or in room, and might return some day.

**Customers are individuals** away from home looking for comfort, rest, familiarity, recognition, and a reason to return some day.

Δ Δ Δ Δ Δ

Clients sit in offices and have meetings in conference rooms.

**Customers are the people** who react to your ideas and appreciate the value you add.

Δ Δ Δ Δ Δ

Patients sit patiently in waiting rooms as they are moved from test to test or room to room.

**Customers are people** scared about their medical conditions and worried for their futures.

Δ Δ Δ Δ Δ

Participants at a conference have paid for their admission and eagerly wait to hear nuggets of brilliance from the speakers.

**Customers are individuals** with important personal concerns seeking new insights and experiences to help them achieve personal and professional goals.

**Customers are PEOPLE** -- treat them humanely and with respect, as they most certainly deserve.

Customers are not "the man in seat 17F," or "the woman in room 839," or "the couple at table 14." And most assuredly, to them, they are also not "seat 17F," or "room 839", or "table 14." Yet, how many times a day do your staff refer to your customers this way (and hence THINK about them this way)?

Customers are "the customer in seat 17F," and "the customer in room 839,' and "the customers at table 14" and they deserve to be spoken about and thought about in this way by your staff and colleagues.

Think of your customers as **CUSTOMERS**. As **PEOPLE**.

And treat them as **CUSTOMERS and PEOPLE**.

Think of them, and treat them, as **CUSTOMERS and PEOPLE** with real and individual needs, wants, and desires. Not as account numbers, participants, account holders, clients, passengers, guests, or patients.

Do this and you will have more customers.

Do this and you will have happier customers.

Do this and you will have repeat customers.

Do this, and your happy and repeat customers will help to ensure a better and more stable future for your organization.

It all starts with how you think about, call, and refer to the **people** who buy your goods and services.

**KEY POINT**: the choice of descriptive can alter the way you and your colleagues think about your customers.

**TAKING ACTION**: for the next week, record every descriptive used internally to describe the people who buy your goods and services. In what context are these words used? How do these words reflect the TRUE feelings of your staff towards your customers? How would their thinking change if the word "customer" had been inserted every time another descriptive was used?

For the next week, review every piece of internal and external communication generated. How often are the people who buy your goods and services described as customers? How often are they described as something else? How do these other words reflect the TRUE feelings of the writers and the readers towards your customers? How would their thinking change if the word "customer" had been used every time another descriptive was used?

Go out to your customer points of interaction. What words are your staff and colleagues using IN FRONT OF CUSTOMERS to describe them? Are your customers being called "room 1027" in front of the customer who is in that room? Are your staff saying "the guy on flight 64 wants to move his seat" in front of the customer making this request?

Start an internal movement now to eliminate ALL descriptive names and words used by your organization other than the word CUSTOMER to refer to the people who buy or use your goods and services.

### #126

# Customer Retention Marketing

Why is customer loyalty so important?

For one thing, numerous research studies have shown that if you can reduce your attrition rate, that is the annualized rate of lost customers, by as little as five percentage points, you can increase your bottom-line profits by anywhere from 25% to 85%.

That's right, just keeping more of the customers you have and preventing them from taking their business elsewhere can have an immediate, positive impact on your bottom line profits.

The reason for the increased profitability from loyal customers is that they stay longer, cost less to serve, provide higher margins, purchase across product lines, have less price sensitivity, and demonstrate near total immunity to your competition.

Many companies measure customer satisfaction, figuring that this directly translates into customer loyalty. While there is a direct correlation between customer satisfaction (particularly complete customer satisfaction) and customer loyalty, managers need to remember that customer satisfaction is an *attitude.*

Relatively high levels of customer satisfaction will not always translate into repeat purchases, particularly in saturated markets and industries, where your customers have many, many alternatives available to them.

Customer loyalty, on the other hand, is a *behavior* that is attained through consistently delivering high levels of complete customer satisfaction.

Another thing to remember is that not all customers are of equal value. Typically, a customer who has been with you for a longer time is more valuable than a more recently acquired customer. For instance, a customer who has been with you for five years is likely to be giving you 8-10 times the *profit* stream of a newly acquired customer.

Hence, if you lose a customer that has been buying from you for five years, you may need to replace that customer with not one, but perhaps eight to ten new customers just to replace the value of this one lost customer.

If there is one message you want to give your staff today, it may be a renewed emphasis on keeping and satisfying the customers you have.

Keeping *good customers* is a more sure-fire method for future success than a constant focus on attracting new customers.

In the past, being customer-oriented has meant operating in order to meet the needs of the typical customer, or the average customer.

Fewer and fewer businesses today can afford to focus on the average customer. Your future growth, and future profitability, comes from *satisfying the needs of your most valuable customers.*

To treat your most valuable customers not as average customers, but as your most valued customers, requires that they be treated as individuals — with individual needs, wants and desires.

This is the true essence of why customer retention is **the art of keeping good customers.**™

**KEY POINT**: your future growth, and future profitability, comes from satisfying the needs of your most valuable customers.

**TAKING ACTION**: can you identify your most important good customers? What criteria do you use to determine who is a good customer and who is not? Why?

What criteria do the people buying your products and services use to classify you as a good supplier? How closely aligned are these criteria with the ones you use in determining good customers? Where are there gaps between the two sets of criteria?

How can you tailor your products and/or services to better meet the needs of your good customers?

What can be done to increase the individual experiences received by your good customers when they interact with your organization?

# More Thoughts on Customer Retention Marketing

In the last two *Monday Morning Marketing Memos*, I have written about customers being hidden assets of an organization.

Hence, you can imagine how aghast I was recently when walking through an airport and coming across a poster for a software company that read:

*"Customers are an investment. Maximize your return."*

Not surprisingly, this company was touting its CRM (customer relationship management) software solutions.

Customers are not an investment!

Customers are the lifeblood of your organization. As Henry Ford once said, "it is not the employer who pays wages, he only handles the money. It is the product that pays wages." If I were to paraphrase Mr. Ford, I would say that "it is the customer who pays wages."

To me, this whole approach to CRM has been wrong. So I was not surprised to see a company that sells CRM software thinking of customers as an investment, rather than as an asset.

Think about it. Customers do not want their relations with organizations "managed" by the other partner in the relationship.

"Managing" a relationship seems like a contradiction in terms. Do you "manage" your relationship with your spouse? Do you "manage" your relationships with your children, your best friends, your colleagues? I should hope not.

Equally as important, do the other parties in these relationships "manage" their relationship with you? I should doubly hope not.

Rather, in each of these personal relationships, you engage in (hopefully) mutually rewarding, forward-looking activities based on two-way, interactive communication.

Why should one's relationship with an organization be any different?

**Customer Relationship Management is a misnomer.**

Which is why it is not surprising that CRM initiatives at many companies have failed. According to an article in CIO magazine in October, "an AMR study shows that, to date, only 16 percent of CRM initiatives have returned value. The balance has been unable to show returns or failed outright."

In the past, most industry articles about CRM talked about the benefits of using this technology to cross-sell existing customers new products and services, in order to "deepen the customer relationship" with the organization. What companies have apparently started to learn is that customers do not define their relationships with organizations based on the number of products or services they purchase from each institution.

Instead, customers define their relationships with organizations on how they are personally treated and by how the products and services delivered meet their individual and unique needs, wants, and desires.

Recently, I have noticed more industry articles discussing the benefits of CRM software and technology as enabling organizations to "sort good clients from bad," as one recent headline in the Australian Financial Review stated. As one article in the AFR's review of CRM software said, "Companies want technology that ensures a flag goes up in customer service when a high-value customer comes in to ensure red-carpet treatment."

With this approach, it seems that some companies are starting to recognize customers as an asset, not an investment on which to maximize returns.

CRM technology should be used to build, earn, reward, and keep good customers loyal to your organization.

Perhaps it is time to change what the acronym CRM stands for. Hence forth, let's forget CRM as we have known it in the past, and start thinking of it as Customer Retention Marketing.

After all, Customer Retention should be *the art of keeping good customers*.™

CRM technology should be used to help you develop and practice this art by being a tool of your Customer Retention Marketing focus and philosophy.

**KEY POINT**: start thinking of CRM as Customer Retention Marketing.

**TAKING ACTION**: what tools do you use for CRM programs? How can these be used better to encourage greater customer retention of your good customers?

Are you trying to *manage* the relationships with your customers? Why? Do you really think customers want to have their relationships with your organization *managed*?

Ask your staff, "Who pays your wages?" If they answer either "the company" or "our products" it may be time for a corporate culture change that embeds an attitude of "customers pay our wages."

**#131**

# Marketing Starts At The Top

Over the holidays there was a short discussion on one of the branding discussion groups about whether marketing is "bottom-up" and branding is "top-down."

In my opinion, both marketing and branding need to be "top-driven," with marketing seen as part of a successful organization's ethos and culture.

Several years ago I created the Five Principles of Customer-Driven Marketing Strategies. The third principle states that marketing is too important to be left only to the marketing department.

Marketing must permeate the entire organization. Thus, it is neither a "top-down" nor a "bottom-up" approach, but one that infuses the whole organization and is inculcated in all internal communications. However, it must be led by senior management.

Marketing — as an ethos and a philosophy for doing business — is central for the survival and prosperity of your organization. This is why it is far too important to be left to only a handful of marketing specialists.

To ensure that this happens, this inculcation and indoctrination of marketing as a philosophy for doing business, combined with the emphasis on understanding customer needs, must be led by the top of the organization.

This point was reinforced to me when reading the monthly newsletter from Copernicus Marketing.

This newsletter (January 2004) discusses why the recent CEOs of McDonald's and Kraft became corporate casualties last year. In the view of the folks at Copernicus Marketing, these two high-profile CEOs were dismissed from their leadership positions because they each created "a marketing vacuum at their respective companies that sucked the life out of their brands and ultimately their careers."

It is obvious, from reading this newsletter, that the leadership at both McDonald's and Kraft lost sight of what their respective customers value in these two brands. Perhaps, now that each is headed by new leaders, these companies can rebound. But to do so will take not only marketing leadership from the top, but the permeation of customer-focused marketing principles and concepts throughout each organization.

Too many CEOs these days see their primary roles as cutter of costs and manipulators of financial figures. I would suggest that these duties be carried out by the Chief Operating Officer. A CEO can better serve his or her customers, employees, communities, board, and shareholders (please note the sequential order of these constituents) by being the guardian of the corporate brand, the motivator of marketing excellence, and the champion of understanding customer needs.

From all appearances, barring any natural or man-made disasters, the majority of the world is entering another economic growth phase. The organizations that take advantage of this the most — the ones which will reap the greatest financial benefits and increased customer shares — from the heady days ahead will be the ones with a marketing focus at the top.

The winners in this next portion of the economic cycle are not going to be the cost cutters and the retrenchers. The winners are going to be the marketing innovators and the ones who protect, and enhance, the values of their brands.

The winners are going to be those whose marketing efforts are led from the top, and who fully understand that *if it touches the customer, it's a marketing issue.*™

**KEY POINT:** the winners in this next portion of the economic cycle are going to be the marketing innovators and the ones who protect, and enhance, the values of their brands.

**TAKING ACTION:** how do you get everybody in your organization involved in understanding customer needs? How do you get everybody in your organization to understand that customers are the *raison d'être* for your business?

What and where are your customer *touch points*? Are these touch points customer-driven or internally process driven?

Do your staff view customers and clients as "problems"? How does your staff react to urgent requests or extraordinary demands by your customers and clients? What can you do to make them understand things from your customers' perspectives so that their attitudes change from customer animosity to a willingness to put in the extra effort required to meet a customer need?

#142

# Complaints Are Good

As sure as there are customers for your product, you can be guaranteed that there will be complaints about your products or services.

Why?

Is it impossible for any organization to deliver 100% customer satisfaction and 100% fault-free products and services all the time? In a simple word: yes.

I have yet to come across an organization that does not make the occasional mistake, or the employee who does not commit the odd accidental error or who simply is in a grumpy mood that is reflected onto your customers.

So face it — complaints will happen.

And this is good. For complaints are good for you.

One of the worst things customers can do when faced with unsatisfactory service or a poor quality product is to not tell you and leave for the competition. After all, if you do not hear of the problems that cause customers to take their business elsewhere, how can you fix them?

Customer complaints are good for these:

- Highlight areas that need improvement.

- Identify procedures that cause customer pain.

- Reveal information that is lacking, or erroneous, in your communications.

- Identify staff who need more training or closer supervision.

- Provide a check on consistency levels.

- Surface policies that may be outdated.

- Trigger positive change (if you take the initiative to act on the complaints).

- Raise staff morale (through positive change).

- Provide a method of competitive intelligence.

- Provide bench marking from other industries.

- Identify customers who care.

That last point is a critical one to ponder. Customers who complain are customers who care!

Sure, customers who complain often want some form of restitution for the inconveniences suffered. But most just want the organization to live up to the promises made, which ought to be the key objective of the selling organization anyway.

So while they care about themselves and having their own satisfaction levels fulfilled, they also care enough about future engagements with the organization to want to help the organization live up to future commitments.

Otherwise, they would simply just walk away and take their business elsewhere (after demanding a refund of whatever money has already been spent on the unsatisfactory product or service).

Whether they are loyal customers, upset customers, wronged customers, disappointed customers, angry customers, right customers, or even wrong customers — customers who complain do care. (Okay, maybe not all, but certainly most.)

If your staff attitudes can be shifted so that they collectively and individually view complainers as customers who care, then your organization is in a much better position to learn from such complaints and to implement restorative steps that result in retrieval of departing and departed customers.

Unfortunately, too many organizations treat customer complaints as "sore points" that need to be counted, rectified, and forgotten as soon as the service staff moves on to the next complaining customer. This is why too much of "customer service" these days is reactionary and process driven, with managers and service staff monitored and measured in terms of efficiencies, quickness of response, and the number of complaints "handled" per shift, day, week, or month.

When complaints are handled and tracked this way, true organizational learning and the opportunity to turn complaints into new levels of customer satisfaction through positive change are usually lost. Forever. Or at least until an enlightened new manager takes over the so-called customer service unit.

Lastly, it is important to remember that all complainers have one of two things in common — they are all customers or prospects.

Service recovery starts with the way you handle complaints and complainers, a topic that we will discuss in the next *Monday Morning Marketing Memo*.

Until then, remember that complaints are good. And that, for the most part, people who complain are customers who truly care about your future. Or at least your future with them as your customers.

**KEY POINT**: customers who complain are customers who care.

**TAKING ACTION**: how are customer complaints handled in your organization? Are they processed and handled as quickly and efficiently as possible, and then forgotten? What steps are needed to turn the efficient handling of customer complaints into learning opportunities for your organization?

How is customer service monitored and measured in your organization? What does your customer service "scorecard" look like? Does it include measurements for how lessons from the frontline are circulated to other staff, used in training courses, and incorporated into new employee orientation programs?

How can lessons from the frontline be turned into learning stories to the benefit of the entire organization and its customers?

# Making It Easy For Customers To Complain

Two of the key points from last week's *Monday Morning Marketing Memo* are:

1) complaints will happen because mistakes will happen, and

2) customers who complain are customers who care.

Therefore, knowing that you are going to get complaints and knowing that such complaints are good for you, it makes sense to have a complaint management strategy in place. Such a complaint management strategy must not only focus on resolving the various customer issues that crop up, but needs to also systematically turn customer complaints into learning opportunities for the entire organization.

The first component of your complaint management strategy is that you should make it easy for customers to complain.

"What?" I can hear many of you saying. "Make it easier for customers to complain, so that we actually get more complaints?"

But that's exactly what your goal should be — to drive more complaints. After all, if you do not hear about the problems your customers are having with your products, services, or staff, then how are you going to go fix these?

Secondly, when a customer has a complaint, and they run into hurdles and barriers trying to voice their complaint to someone, all they do is get angrier and angrier. This results in a small problem developing into a multi-faceted larger one, simply because the customer cannot find a way to channel their concerns, anger, fears, worries, questions, or complaints to your organization in a timely and convenient manner.

This is particularly true when it comes to the information posted on your website. Few things seem to infuriate customers more these days than not being able to find the right contact details for lodging a complaint, or for speaking to someone other than a call center "service rep" on an organization's website.

Thus, there are two key benefits from making it easy for customers to complain:

1) The customers do not get angrier and more upset from the additional frustrations of trying to contact your organization.

2) You have more opportunities to fix initial, small problems before they evolve into larger and harder to resolve ones.

Part of your complaint management strategy needs to emphasize to all employees, especially the first tier and second tier staff who routinely have to deal with 90% of customer complaints, that service recovery starts with how they react to complaints.

Unfortunately, for too many organizations the initial reaction to a customer complaint is either defensive (trying to push the blame back onto the customer) or process driven (having a focus on a speedy resolution so that the frontline service staff can rapidly move onto the next customer complaint).

This approach often has unintended negative consequences, as customers end up feeling that they have been handled in a non-personalized fashion or have been quickly served so that another customer's situation can take priority. This is not to say that speed and prompt resolutions are not appreciated; however it is important to understand that the manner in which swift results are delivered can be perceived as dehumanizing and robotic.

A good example of this is when an organization's email auto responder system sends out the highly depersonalizing "thank you for your enquiry, we will get back to you promptly" message when an email of complaint is sent via the organization's website.

Please note: an email (or letter) of complaint is not an enquiry. It is an attempt to get a humanized and customized resolution to a situation that your customer finds unpalatable. It should not be responded to in the same manner as an email asking a general product or service question.

Additionally, in the most unfortunate situations, another unintended negative consequence of the focus on speed is that the customer actually walks away feeling unheard and that his or her true, underlining complaint was ignored, overlooked, or not fully understood. The result is that customers feel it is difficult to voice their complaints to the organization, and may end up deciding that it is far easier to take their business elsewhere than to continue dealing with an organization that fails to listen and comprehend.

It is for this reason that I advocate changing "*customer service staff*" into "**customer satisfaction staff**," who are then measured on their abilities to deliver complete satisfaction to customers, rather than by quantitative indicators such as the number of calls handled, the number of customers served, and the average time per service transaction.

This is not a matter of semantics, but of a philosophical approach of being fully customer focused and pro-active in the area of customer satisfaction, rather than being reactive and process driven in determining customer service standards.

One interesting thing I have noticed is that customers are more acute listeners and observers when they are angry. In fact, when angered customers notice every little detail about how they are being treated and what steps the organization is taking to settle the dispute. As a result, each and every thing done by someone representing the organization, including outsourced contract staff such as those in call centers, is noted and mentally recorded by upset customers. This is especially true for any attempts to forestall the customer from complaining or to thwart their desires to be fully heard and understood.

Customers willingly play these details back to the next level of management, or to anyone else who will listen — including your other customers and prospects — at a moment's notice. This not only lengthens the time it takes to eventually solve the original customer complaint, but it also means the dissatisfactions incurred by the customer while engaged in the settlement process must now also be dealt with. This leads to additional costs to the organization, in terms of both staff hours and the eventual compensation to the customer, as well as an unsatisfying feeling all around for the customer, your staff, and the management personnel involved.

All this could be alleviated, of course, if you simply made it easier for customers to complain in the first place.

One of my personal marketing cornerstones is that preventing customer complaints is better than resolving them. Such prevention, however, must come through quality products, services, procedures, processes, policies, and staff. This does not imply that you should prevent customer complaints from being fully voiced and understood.

When something goes wrong, it is best to hear about it. Only the problems your organization hears and knows about are fixable.

Handling customer complaints properly impacts all current and future customers — and starts with processes, procedures, and systems that make it easy for such complaints to be communicated to your organization.

So, make it easy and convenient for your customers to complain. You will be glad you did. For the benefits will be for you and the organization to reap.

**KEY POINT**: make it easy for customers to complain to your organization.

**TAKING ACTION**: how are customer complaints handled in your organization? Are they processed and handled as quickly and efficiently as possible, and then forgotten? What can be done so that customer complaints are fully voiced and understood?

What steps are needed to turn the efficient handling of complaints into learning opportunities for your organization?

How is customer service monitored and measured in your organization? What does your customer service "scorecard" look like? Does it include measurements for how lessons from the frontline points of customer interaction are circulated to other staff, used in training courses, and incorporated into new employee orientation programs?

# Complaints Management: The AGREEMENT Model

Handling customer complaints is an art that combines tact and diplomacy with a structured process that involves both the customer and the organization.

Too often, however, the customer is not involved in this process, other than at the start by actually complaining and at the end by agreeing (or not agreeing) to accept the resolution proffered by the organization.

When teaching supervisory skills to managers, trainers put an emphasis on the need to *involve subordinates* in the decision-making process in order to achieve individual and group buy-in. A fundamental principle of good people management is that *individuals and groups have greater buy-in when they are involved in the decision-making process.*

Unfortunately, this principle is rarely applied to the field of customer service. As a result, customer service is seen as an "internal" matter. Once a resolution has been agreed upon internally by frontline personnel and management, then the proposed solution is presented or "sold" to the customer for their acceptance or rejection.

I firmly believe, however, that if a complaining customer is involved in the process of determining a resolution to their complaint, two things will occur:

a) the customer and the organization will both have a greater buy-in for the agreed upon solution, and

b) the bonds of loyalty between the customer and the organization will be strengthened.

With this in mind, I created the AGREEMENT Model for effective complaints handling.

This 9-step procedure includes Acknowledgement, Gracious, Research, Explore, Evaluate, Mirror, Explain, Notify, and Train.

In implementing the AGREEMENT method, the organization should:

**Acknowledge** that the customer has a legitimate issue (from their perspective) and that this situation provides an opportunity to understand and eliminate a problem, error, mistake, or other factors that may cause future customer complaints.

Be **Gracious** in accepting the customer complaint and *thank the customer* for the feedback received.

Conduct **Research** into the true nature of the complaint by *asking the customer questions* on how the situation arose, how the customer's expectations were developed, and how the customer sees the shortfall between their expectations and what they feel they received. Then, all the relevant staff members involved in the product or service situation need to be asked the same questions, including what they thought the customer's expectations were and whether they feel they delivered upon these expectations.

Engage the customer in a dialogue to **Explore** possible solutions to the situation, and then explore these same ideas internally to determine which can feasibly be delivered without compounding the customer's frustrations and dissatisfaction.

**Evaluate** the various solution options *with the customer* and ascertain which one is most likely to resolve the situation to the satisfaction of the customer.

**Mirror** the customer at *all times*. If the customer has communicated their complaint informally, then respond using the same medium (phone, email, fax, face-to-face) that the customer has used. If the customer has made a more formal complaint, then respond likewise and from someone in the organization *that the customer* will consider to be at an appropriate level.

**Explain** to the customer what the research has uncovered as to the true causes behind what led to their complaint. Be honest and forthright, without being accusatory or assigning individual blame.

**Notify** the customer of the steps that will be taken to resolve the situation and the expected timeframe in which this will occur.

Use the situation to **Train** *everybody in the organization,* include future new hires, to help prevent a similar occurrence with another customer in the future. (Note: too often organizations use customer complaints as a training and coaching tool only for those involved in the specific situation, which means that other customers make the same complaints because the problem has not been eliminated from *the entire organization).*

As you can see, the AGREEMENT Model aims to keep the customer involved throughout the complaint resolution process. By getting the customer involved in the processing of resolving their complaint, the organization has a greater chance of obtaining buy-in and commitment from the customer for the solution chosen.

An additional benefit is that often the idea for the resolution comes from the customer. This not only speeds up the resolution process for this particular customer, but it also gives the organization a new idea for how to handle other customer complaints or, better yet, how to prevent future customer problems.

Complaining customers are not the enemy. Treat them with respect, grace, and concern, and get them involved in the resolution process, and you can turn a negative situation and an upset customer into a long-lasting relationship with a loyal customer.

**KEY POINT**: if a complaining customer is involved in the process of determining a resolution to their complaint, then two things occur: a) the customer and the organization will both have a greater buy-in for the agreed upon solution, and b) the bonds of loyalty between the customer and the organization will be strengthened.

**TAKING ACTION:** whenever you receive a customer complaint be sure to thank the customer for their feedback and use this situation as an opportunity to re-dedicate your staff to eliminating the problems, errors, mistakes, and other factors that cause customer complaints rather than trying to just eliminate the complaints themselves.

Teach your staff to be gracious in receiving customer complaints and to acknowledge that the customer has a legitimate issue (from their perspective) that needs to be satisfactorily resolved.

Keep the customer involved in the resolution determining process. By asking questions of the customer staff have a better chance of uncovering the true nature of the complaint. By exploring solution options with the customer the organization has a greater chance of obtaining buy-in and commitment from the customer for the solution chosen.

Use all major customer complaints as a teaching and coaching tool for all staff and all new hires so that errors and mistakes are not replicated in other parts of the operation.

#151

# The Four PEs of Customer Loyalty

One of the biggest drawbacks of the now-famous Four Ps of Marketing (product, price, promotion, and place) is that marketers and managers use these four topics as internally focused management tools, thereby losing the opportunity to focus on the customer and the customer experience in the equation.

In recent months, as I have been researching and organizing my next book (tentatively titled *Customer Retention: The Art of Keeping Good Customers*™), I have been giving a great deal of thought to the importance of the various experiences that customers receive when selecting, purchasing, and using products and services. Since each of these experiences has an impact on whether or not the customer repeats business with the selling organization, each therefore has a direct impact on customer loyalty.

Thus far I have categorized these experiences into four, which I now refer to as the Four PEs of customer loyalty:

Promise/Performance Experiences

People Experiences

Process Experiences

Personal Experiences

Customers, whether they are individual consumers or business-to-business clients, are in a perpetual state of *experience evaluation* of your products, services, brands, and organizations. These evaluations are conducted at both a conscious and subconscious level on an on-going basis, not just when customers are in the so-called buying cycle.

Since customers are constantly evaluating their experiences with your products, services, brands and organization, so should you. And I do mean constantly, not just on a quarterly, annual, or other periodic basis.

To be customer-focused in action, rather than just in word, means understanding the experiences that customers have as a result of doing business with you and how this impacts their lives, both positively and negatively.

Sure, lots of companies talk about being customer-centric, customer-focused, or even customer centered. But in most cases, that is exactly what it is — all talk.

Or, with some more enlightened companies, it actually results in a bit of flexibility, a bit of customization, and an attempt to provide meaningful options to customers.

Am I being too harsh? Ask yourself the question I have asked myself many times: can you name a dozen companies that you deal with that are truly customer focused, from your perspective, and that succeed on all four PE points? Can you name half-a-dozen companies that you deal with that are truly customer focused and loyal to you as a customer? (If you can, please send me your lists and tell me why, these might be good case study candidates for my next book.)

In my case, the answer to the first question includes Amazon, Australian Post, Avis, Cape Lodge (a luxury boutique hotel in Margaret River), Coca-Cola, Create Space (owned by Amazon), and Singapore Post. While your experiences may differ, Amazon, Avis, Coca-Cola, and the two national postal services have been consistently reliable across all four categories for me.

But note, not a single airline, bank, or hotel chain makes my list, despite the fact that I have numerous relationships with several organizations in each of these categories.

# The Best of the Monday Morning Marketing Memo

Qantas almost makes my list, but falls down with regards to the constant unavailability of seats using frequent flyer points and the unfriendly rules (from a customer's perspective) and restrictions they have on how FFP points can be used for upgrades and free seats. Qantas also fails often at getting priority luggage up on the baggage belt before other bags, including crew member bags!

And Singapore Airlines succeeds on the last three categories, but consistently falls down with regards to performance experiences received on board, especially in terms of food and wine choices.

Interestingly, I have banking relationships with eight different institutions in three countries, and yet not one of these is truly customer focused from this customer's perspective. (Perhaps that is why I maintain eight different relationships, rather than consolidating all my business with one financial institution.)

Is it a small wonder that so few companies seem capable of creating true customer loyalty? Perhaps this is because most are more interested in creating quarterly profit figures that excite institutional investors instead of experiences that excite individual customers.

Is it a small wonder that so few customers feel loyal to their product or service providers? Companies and marketers often complain that there is no loyalty in customers any more. Yet I challenge them to tell me, and their customers, why they deserve customer loyalty. When I asked them to itemize the things they do that should result in customer loyalty, I usually receive very short lists topped with a few areas in which they believe they deliver upon their promises.

What these companies do not understand is that delivering upon what they promise is only the starting point for building and earning customer loyalty.

I suggest that you and your colleagues give serious thought to the various experiences that your customers receive when selecting, purchasing, and using your products and services. Each of these experiences has an impact on whether or not your customers are likely to repeat business with your organization.

**KEY POINT**: customers, whether they are individual consumers or business-to-business clients, are in a perpetual state of *experience evaluation* of your products, services, brands, and organizations.

**TAKING ACTION**: make a list of all the things your organization does that you think should result in customer loyalty. How well does the organization consistently deliver against the points on this list?

Randomly survey some customers, particularly some of your larger customers, and ask them to rate the points on your list from most important to least important. What do these results tell you about how your customers view the importance of each item on your customer loyalty building list?

Ask your customers to specify items and actions that are missing from your list.

Evaluate your organization's performance against all Four PEs of Customer Loyalty. What needs fixing? What can be leveraged?

# Taking Care of Customers

I was in Melbourne in mid August (1999) attending a major meeting of the Australian and New Zealand banks that issue MasterCard credit cards and Maestro debit cards.

Mr. Nicholas Utton, Chief Marketing Officer of MasterCard International at that time, had one key message for this audience of senior bankers concerning customers: "*if we don't take care of our customers, someone else will.*"

That's worth repeating --- and reflecting on: **"if we don't take care of our customers, someone else will."**

And how true that is.

Just think about all the choices and options available to your customers today.

Rare is the organization that finds itself without numerous competitors. Even rarer is the customer without readily available options, choices, or substitute products for the solutions they seek.

To take care of your customers, you need to have a full understanding of their wants, needs, and desires.

I would also suggest that you need to have a corporate-wide attitude that understands a person or an organization is not truly your customer until the second time they buy.

That is right. I recommend you do not consider anyone a customer until the second time they buy from you.

The first time they buy they are merely a trial user. Unless they achieve satisfaction from the purchase and the use of your product or service, they may be unlikely to repeat their business with you.

Hence, taking care of the customer goes beyond the mere sales cycle and includes all post-purchase activities such as use, repair, servicing, customer service, warranties, and trade-in or re-sale.

The best way to take care of your prospects and customers is to tailor or customize your products and service offerings as much as you profitably can.

Treat your customers as individuals — with individual needs — at all customer touch points and you will be well on your way to developing customer loyalty.

And remember, in the words of MasterCard's former Chief Marketing Officer, if you don't take care of your customers, someone else will.

**KEY POINT**: if you don't take care of your customers, someone else will.

**TAKING ACTION**: are you fully aware of the experiences customers have with your products? How satisfying are these experiences? Any way to find out?

Where can your product or service offer be customized? How can you create tailored solutions for your very, very important customers?

How can you find out if a first-time customer is likely to buy from you again?

#156

# Customer Retention:
# The Art of Keeping Good Customers

The world in which marketing takes place has changed, and continues to change at a rapid pace.

Customers, customer needs, and the motivations for making purchasing decisions are also changing.

Plus, the natural loyalty of customers is a thing of the past, not just because customers have become more fickle but also because the large majority of organizations do not exhibit any tendencies that deserve customer loyalty.

As customers become more knowledgeable about the options available to them, as well as more aware and understanding about their own individual wants, needs, and desires, the more they want to be recognized and understood as individuals. Without a doubt, customers will give their business — and more important their repeat business - to the organizations that do the best job of understanding and responding to their individual wants, needs, and desires.

In this highly competitive marketing environment, organizations need to move from a transaction-focus and product-line focus to a customer focus. Highly successful firms of the future will take this a step further, by developing techniques to continuously learn from interactions with customers. They will then implement procedures that enable them to deepen customer relationships by properly responding to the insights gained from these interactions.

Early attempts at this direction have often gone wrong, for the simple reason that the global CRM movement convinced senior executives that customer relationships could be managed. No customer that I have ever spoken with wants to have their relationship with a selling organization managed. The whole concept of taking an economic view of customers that measures the profitability of each individual customer and then attempting to manage (i.e. grow) those relationships that the organization finds to be profitable is, at best, one-sided and valid for short durations only.

In the confusion of these highly expensive, technology-led CRM implementations, customer relationships were defined by product ownership levels, size of orders, and cross-selling opportunities. While all valid parameters from an organization's perspective, none of these are the key ways in which customers would primarily define their relationships with the organizations with which they do business.

Additionally, from a customer's perspective, they want their relationships to be nurtured, cultivated, appreciated, cherished, and looked after. Anything but managed!

One of my personal goals for the coming year is to help organizational leaders move beyond the primeval and self-centered goals currently being practiced in many operations to a business philosophy that is more likely to help retain the customer relationships critical to continued success. At the heart of this philosophy, which I call *the art of keeping good customers,*™ is the changing of the acronym CRM to mean Customer Retention Marketing.

Customer retention has a direct impact on corporate profitability. As one often-cited report in the Harvard Business Review showed, a decrease of just five percentage points in customer attrition can increase bottom-line profitability by 25% to 80% across a wide range of industries.

How important is the issue of customer retention? Another Harvard Business Review article stated that "the average U.S. corporation loses one-half of their customers every five years and these (attrition) rates stunt corporate growth by up to 35 percent."

It is little wonder that an Economist Intelligent Unit article *Managing Customer Relationships* reported that "the number of businesses citing 'customer retention' as a critically important measure in the next five years has jumped to nearly 60%, as companies shift their focus from attracting new customers to retaining their more profitable ones."

This means your own customer base is a highly under-valued asset.

Successful companies today are switching from a transaction perspective with their customers to a customer loyalty-building perspective. The way to do this is to earn customer loyalty by understanding true customer needs, committing to quality, delivering upon the promises you make, and by treating customers as people, not as accounts.

In the past, being customer–oriented has meant operating in order to meet the needs of the typical customer, or the average customer.

Fewer and fewer businesses today can afford to focus on the average customer. Your future growth, and future profitability, comes from satisfying the needs of your most valuable customers.

To treat your most valuable customers not as average customers, but as your most valued customers, requires that they be treated as individuals — each having individual needs, wants, desires, likes, and dislikes.

This is the true essence behind the concept of the *art of keeping good customers.*™

**KEY POINT**: fewer and fewer businesses can afford to focus on the average customer; you need to treat your most valuable customers not as average customers but as your most valued customers.

**TAKING ACTION**: does your organization respect your customers and prospects, or do you see them in terms of the transactions they make with you?

Do you appreciate that your customers seek convenience and do you have the processes in place that enhance convenience to your customers?

Are you in the business of solving problems for your customers, or merely in the business of making products and hoping that someone purchases these?

**#159**

# A New Definition of Marketing

It is with shock and horror that I read recently that an Australian Marketing Institute white paper titled *What Value Marketing?* describes "the ultimate role of marketing as delivering increased shareholder value."

When and how did our industry get so far off the mark?

Contrast this with the new definition of marketing from the American Marketing Association, unveiled in the middle of last year:

> "Marketing is an organizational function and a set of processes for creating, communicating and delivering value to customers and for managing

customer relationships in ways that benefit the organization and its stakeholders."

It is rather sad that even the American Marketing Association (AMA) definition talks about managing customer relationships only in terms of benefits to the organization and its stakeholders. After all, if the customer does not benefit from the relationship, I can guarantee you the relationship will not last very long.

Using the new American Marketing Association version as a base, my preferred definition of marketing has become:

"Marketing is an organization-wide function and a set of disciplined processes for the creation, communication, and delivery of value to customers. The ultimate role of marketing is to create and keep good customers, for the benefit of customers, the organization, and stakeholders."

As I wrote last week, business is not just about sales, contracts, cash flow, internal rates of return, and profitability. Even Henry Ford recognized this when he said, "a business that makes nothing but money is a poor kind of business."

Marketing — as an ethos and a philosophy for doing business — is central for the survival and prosperity of any organization. This is why it is far too important to be left to only a handful of marketing specialists.

Marketing must permeate the entire organization and is not something that should be seen as either a "top-down" or a "bottom-up" approach, but one that infuses the whole organization. This inculcation and indoctrination of marketing as a philosophy for doing business, combined with the emphasis on understanding customer needs and creating value for customers, must be led by the top of the organization.

## The Best of the Monday Morning Marketing Memo

Too many CEOs and other senior executives these days see their primary roles as cutters of costs and manipulators of financial figures.

A CEO can better serve his or her customers, employees, communities, board, and shareholders (please note the sequential order of these constituents) by being the guardian of the corporate brand, the motivator of marketing excellence, and the champion of understanding customer needs.

Likewise, marketing also needs to become a central concern of Boards of Directors. Here is what William Parrett, Chief Executive at Deloitte Touche Tohmatsu, wrote in the December 11, 2004 issue of The Economist:

*"A recent survey by Deloitte and the Economist Intelligence Unit found that management and boards of directors focus far too much on financial results*

*that represent lagging indicators of past performance. We believe they should pay far more attention to non-financial factors such as customer satisfaction, product and service quality, operational performance, and employee commitment — leading indicators of future performance that firms can use to navigate confidently toward a sustainable future. We also encourage corporate management to communicate with stakeholders about these indicators in quarterly and annual reports."*

The winners in this next segment of the economic cycle are not going to be the cost cutters and the retrenchers. The winners are going to be the marketing innovators and the ones who create, protect, and enhance the values customers receive and perceive from transacting business with them and from being associated with them.

It is not only your sales force that must create value for your customers. It is your entire organization. Our personal marketing philosophy is *if it touches the customer, it's a marketing issue.*™

Everything your organization does touches your customers and your prospects. Hence, everything you do not only is marketing related, but also impacts the results of your marketing efforts.

In fact, if anything your organization is doing does not add value to your customers or is hurting your competition, then why are you doing it?

In short, everything you do should be done to create value for customers.

This is how you create and keep good customers. Creating and keeping good customers will enable your organization to achieve its bottom-line financial goals, and to increase shareholder value.

But you have to take care of your customers first. As Lee Iacocca, former Chairman and CEO of Chrysler, is quoted as saying "if you take care of your customers, everything else will fall into place."

And that is why my definition of marketing is focused on customers first, the organization second, and shareholders third.

**KEY POINT**: the ultimate role of marketing is to create and keep good customers, to the benefit of customers, the organization, and stakeholders.

**TAKING ACTION**: review your mission statement. Is the emphasis on your customers, the organization, employees, or shareholders? If the answer is anything other than customers, now would be a good time to create a new mission statement.

How involved is your Board in your marketing activities? What steps can be taken to get the Board more interested in marketing and other leading-edge factors such as customer satisfaction, product and service quality, operational performance, and employee commitment?

What role does marketing play in your organization? Is it confined to a solitary functional department? What would it take to create a marketing ethos that permeated your entire organization?

**#163**

# Protecting Your Corporate Brand

Ever since I wrote my first book in 1997, *Corporate Image Management: A Marketing Discipline for the 21st Century,* I have advocated that "**nothing touches the customer more than how he or she perceives your corporate image**."

Corporate image management, or what some writers and researchers refer today as corporate reputation management, remains one of the most important (and yet most overlooked) management and marketing disciples for businesses, organizations, associations, and government entities.

# The Best of the Monday Morning Marketing Memo

In today's global market environment, customer trust in organizations, particularly corporations, is at an all-time low as a direct fallout from the never-ending series of widely reported scandals (i.e. WorldCom and CEO Bernie Ebbers, Enron, Martha Stewart, HIH Insurance, OneTel, Tyco, Citicorp's recent activities in Japan and Europe, Boeing, and Parmalat in Italy).

Corporate image management has always been important, but perhaps never as important as today. As Federal Reserve Chairman Alan Greenspan said in his Commencement Address at Harvard University in 1999, "In today's world, where ideas are increasingly displacing the physical in the production of economic value, competition for reputation becomes a significant driving force, propelling our economy forward."

The corporate image is an extremely important corporate asset, one deserving the same attention and commitment by senior management as any other vital issue. The key to managing this asset is to fully understand that your stakeholders' perceptions embody your corporate image.

Unfortunately for every organization, these stakeholder perceptions are no longer (and I doubt if they truly ever were) formed solely through experiences with your products and services.

For instance, a multiyear study by Cone Inc., a marketing and communications firm based in Boston, reveals that American customers are now increasingly taking into consideration the reputation and track record of social responsibility of the companies they will keep in their spending circle. Eighty percent reportedly said corporate support of a cause is a key factor in whether or not they trust a particular firm, an increase of 21 percent from the previous year.

According to Carol Cone, CEO of Cone, "This study, a series of research spanning over a decade, shows that in today's climate, more than ever before, companies must get involved with social issues in order to protect and enhance their reputations."

Supporting a cause can improve a company's status with customers. Companies that are caught or reported behaving unethically or illegally can also expect to receive some clearly defined customer responses. In such cases, according to the Cone research:

- 90 percent said they would consider switching to another company's product or service.
- 81 percent said they would speak out against the company to family and friends.
- 80 percent would consider selling any stock holdings in the company.

- 80 percent would refuse to invest in the company.

- 75 percent would refuse to work for that company.

- 73 percent said they would boycott that company's goods or services.

- 67 percent said they would be less loyal in their job at that company.

On the other hand, positive corporate activity in social and community issues can have an immediate positive impact on corporate brand images. GMIPoll conducted a survey with 20,000 consumers in 20 countries one week after the South Asian Tsunami, measuring their opinions on American multinational brands, corporate tsunami relief efforts, and U.S. foreign policy. A remarkable 59% of these consumers reported that their impressions of corporate brands improved as a result of the tsunami relief efforts from U.S.-based multinational corporations.

For example, Coca-Cola provided bottled drinking water, basic foodstuffs, and medical supplies to tsunami victims; Starbucks made an initial contribution of $100,000 to international relief organizations CARE and Oxfam UK, plus donated $2 per pound of Sumatra coffee sold during January; and the Bill & Melinda Gates Foundation pledged an initial $3 million to nongovernmental organizations to aid tsunami relief efforts.

The GMIPoll results indicated that as a result of Coke's contributions, 61% of consumers reported an improved image of Coca-Cola. Starbuck's tsunami relief pledge resulted in 51% of respondents expressing an improved image of Starbucks. The Bill and Melinda Gates donation resulted in 50% of respondents reporting an improved image of Microsoft.

Furthermore, 46% of all consumers indicated that they will purchase more products from the companies that provided tsunami relief. For example, 39% indicated they would consider purchasing more Coca-Cola products in the future; 32% indicated they would buy more at Starbucks; and 37% indicated a greater willingness to buy Microsoft products.

Positive brand sentiment gained from tsunami relief efforts stands in stark contrast to images heavily influenced by U.S. foreign policy. The GMIPoll found that one in five international consumers consciously avoids purchasing American brands as a way of displaying their discontent over recent American foreign policies and military action (the three countries with the highest percentage of consumers who indicate an intention to boycott iconic American brands are South Korea 45%, Greece 40% and France 25%).

Softening the blow however, 56% of those who indicated that they consider boycotting American brands also reported that their judgment of those corporations that had donated to the tsunami relief effort had improved; similarly, 48% stated that they would consider purchasing products in the future from those brands that had provided tsunami aid. Clearly, there are powerful international cross currents influencing global consumers' views of American iconic brands.

Corporate branding is more than just positive media coverage, good financial results, and increased market share. And it is certainly more than just donating money, products, or services when natural disasters strike.

Properly managed, your corporate brand should discourage unethical behavior throughout the organization, reduce staff turnover, reduce customer churn and attrition, and minimize negative media coverage. This will happen only when management sees the corporate image as a management discipline, and not just a marketing tool, a graphic design project, or a public relations exercise.

The essential role that corporate image now performs is also a result of major shifts in the field of marketing combined with more knowledgeable and interested customers. The corporate brand image is much more than a name or logo. Your corporate brand reflects your way of doing business, a key component of reputation and identity.

The strongest corporate brands tend to be the ones with the most consistent and clearest messages. These brands create expectations and anticipations in the minds of both consumers who buy, use, or recommend the brands and the employees who deliver upon these inherent promises.

Every organization has a corporate image, whether it wants one or not.

When properly designed and managed, the corporate image will accurately reflect the organization's commitment to quality, excellence, and its relationships with its various constituents: such as current and potential customers, employees and future staff, competitors, partners, governing bodies, and the general public.

Also, when properly managed and communicated, the corporate image will create an internal culture that is more likely to protect the brand and reputation of the organization.

In a sense, this is complete circle of corporate brand protection. A properly managed corporate image creates a culture that protects the brand and reputation, which therefore reinforces and strengthens the management of the corporate image.

This makes the management of your corporate image one of the most potent marketing and management tools available for your senior executives to use in ensuring the viable execution of your corporate vision, as well as ensuring the protection of this most vital corporate asset.

**KEY POINT:** nothing touches the customer more than how he or she perceives your corporate image.

**TAKING ACTION:** who is in charge of your corporate image? If the answer is not "everyone in the organization," then take time to reflect on why not.

When was the last time your senior management team reviewed and discussed your corporate image? How soon can this subject be added to the next senior management meeting agenda?

Survey the top 20% of your customers on their perceptions of your corporate image. Survey 100% of your employees asking the same questions. Compare the results.

#166

# 7 Laws of Customer Retention Marketing

I have long struggled with the concept of Customer Relationship Management (CRM), mostly for the simple reason that I fully understand that customers do not want their relationships with an organization "managed."

This is why the whole notion and philosophy of CRM as customer relationship management is wrong.

In my keynote speech later today at the Services Marketing Conference in Kuala Lumpur, one of my key messages will be that marketers and senior management really need to think of CRM as Customer Retention Marketing.

This is what true CRM is all about - retaining customers, or as I like to call it *the art of keeping good customers.*™

To implement this definition of CRM in your organization, you will need to inculcate the following 7 Laws of Customer Retention Marketing into your culture, processes, and thinking:

1. The conversion of a prospect to a purchaser is the casting of a potential long-term relationship with a possible customer. A purchaser who buys from you the first time is merely a trial user. A customer is not a true customer until the second time they buy from you. Forget the notions that "the relationship starts with a purchase," or "you are not closing a sale, you are starting a relationship." As we pointed out in last week's *Monday Morning Marketing Memo,* the relationship starts way back in the

information seeking stage of the buying cycle, at least from the customer's perspective.

The art of keeping good customers means that your entire organization should be geared to ensure that every experience received by a customer (including a first-time purchaser) should result in that customer repeating their future purchases from you whenever you have a product or solution that meets their needs or solves a problem for them.

2. You do not work for your employer — you work for your customers. Sure, someone in the company signs your proverbial paycheck (or authorizes the direct deposit into your account). But those checks and deposits would bounce if it were not for the customers who buy from your organization. When someone asks you "who do you work for?" your

reply should be "our customers" or "the customers of (name of organization)."

3. You do not sell products or services —you sell solutions that meet the needs, wants, and desires of your customers. As pithy as this sounds, it is something that way too many organizations and workers these days just do not seem to understand.

4. Customers want relationships with people and organizations they trust, that are committed to them, and with whom they have shared goals. All of us can buy products and services from a vast number of suppliers and outlets. But we choose to have continual relationships, and to repeat our business, with those we trust and with those whom we have shared outcomes.

5. Employees should be liberated — and allowed to be customer champions. Almost all staff want to serve customers well, if only their organizations would

let them! Unfortunately many organizations have rules, processes, procedures, and policies that tie the hands of their employees and prevent them from truly serving customers and satisfying their wants, needs, and desires.

6. Do not have a commitment to customer service — have a commitment to customers (and to customer care). We are definitely in the age of the customer. Customers have many choices and options available to them. But they also all share a deficit of sufficient time. Caring about customers means committing to the things customers place high value on — flexibility, sufficient knowledge and information, convenience, ability to choose functions relevant to them, customization, and environmental concerns.

And, of course, good service, which in today's world is now a prerequisite for repeat business as customers will simply not put up with bad service, inconvenience, inflexible policies and procedures, and a lack of options for customization and personalization.

7. Customer Service staff should be fired — and replaced with Customer Satisfaction staff. This is not a matter of semantics. Customer service tends to be either reactive (to a situation) or a follow-up activity (to a complaint).

Customer service, which is problem resolution focused, is usually initiated by the customer, when he or she has a problem. On the other hand, customer satisfaction is proactive and is customer focused.

Customer satisfaction is usually initiated by the organization to improve the quality of the relationship with the customer. The corollary of this rule is that customer service scorecards, measurements, and matrixes should be replaced with indices that measure and monitor customer satisfaction.

In the typical CRM thinking found today, the organization is the center of focus, thinking, and planning. And the measurement tools used are indicators that support managerial bonuses.

In my Customer Retention Marketing model, the customer is the focus and occupies the central platform for all thinking, planning, and strategic focus. The result becomes the optimization of customer-first processes and the continued improvement in the quality of customer interactions.

Your organization will accomplish a great deal more, and be more highly successful, by changing your definition of CRM to Customer Retention Marketing.

**KEY POINT**:  change your definition of CRM to mean Customer Retention Marketing.

**TAKING ACTION**:  survey your employees and ask them this open ended question: "what do we sell to customers?" If they give you a long list of products and services it is time to educate them that you are selling solutions, not products and services.

Review the tools and measurements you use to track and monitor customer service. How could these be turned into tools and measurements to track and monitor customer satisfaction?

# The Best of the Monday Morning Marketing Memo

Prepare an entire issue of your next employee newsletter (or staff memo) on the subject of customer retention marketing, and what the implications are for the organization in terms of customer care, customer satisfaction measurements, liberating of customer contact personnel, changes in policies and procedures, and how you will reward the organization for making the change to customer retention marketing.

# Service Statesmanship

Why do some companies seem to exude stellar service at all levels, when others only offer satisfying service on a sporadic basis?

Outstanding service appears to be inculcated in numerous organizations, and dismally lacking in others. What is the underlying factor that determines whether excellent service delivery is a cultural characteristic of an organization? I think the root cause is the concept of Service Statesmanship.

One of the best definitions of Service Statesmanship came from a CEO who said, "When a fish stinks, it stinks from the head." What he meant, of course, is that service excellence is first and foremost the responsibility of managers and senior executives. Staff, by themselves, cannot ensure excellent service.

After all, when service "stinks," it stinks from the top of the organization right through to the bottom rungs. To stop the rot managers and senior executives need to become Service Statesmen.

When the fish "doesn't stink," managers are usually doing two things. They are establishing service quality and service excellence as the overriding goals of their business units, and they are serving as role models who translate these core values into exemplary personal behavior. These are the key duties of anyone who aspires to be a Service Statesman.

As a role model, a Service Statesman:

- Constantly reinforces the service message to staff, colleagues and peers.

- Constantly communicates the organization's service performance to all staff.

- Holds regular service progress reviews:

  - To review performance against goals.

  - To discuss how to remedy situations where standards are not being met.

## Serving As A Role Model

A Service Statesman is a role model, constantly reinforcing the organization's key service messages and service values.

Having established quality as a high-priority objective, Service Statesmen will literally take this company goal and run with it. They will inspire and cajole other managers to sign up for the program. They will reward their own staff for outstanding service performances. And, many Service

Statesmen will adamantly insist that every executional detail within his or her business unit contributes to every customer's perception of quality service.

This last trait sometimes leads employees to think their managers are "a little crazy about service." This is not bad. Actually, this is good!

The manager who holds up introduction of a new product because the frontline staff have not been fully informed or trained on the product is a Service Statesman. The unit head helping his business unit work out of a processing backlog is a Service Statesman. The branch manager who regularly spot checks account applications for accuracy is a Service Statesman.

A Service Statesman will be seen by staff as constantly engaged and interested in improving service delivery.

# The Best of the Monday Morning Marketing Memo

At one major utility, employees were shocked to see their CEO bicycle to the site of emergency weekend repairs to "spur the troops on" and to motivate those working on the problem. Here was a smart Service Statesman at work, capitalizing on the value of a dramatic gesture and its rapid incorporation into company folklore.

Service Statesmen typically work hard to ensure all service employees correctly interpret decisions affecting operating conditions. During interviews at institutions renowned for service excellence, a large number of managers volunteered examples when they personally explained service policy changes far down the chain of command, even at stressful times on major internal changes.

Seasonal peaks, a new product introduction, or customers leaving for a major competitor — any of these planned or unplanned events can swamp employees with extraordinary service burdens. Certainly managers should give employees all the practical assistance possible during such stressful periods, but at the same time managers must reinforce the organization's corporate service values and reward peak or superior individual performance, especially those performed in times of duress.

In short, managers who desire to be Service Statesmen must:

- take a personally active role in building service excellence into the organization,

- establish service excellence and quality customer service as the over-riding goal in their business units, and

- serve as a role model through exemplary personal behavior at all times.

Service quality delivery has strategic importance for the long-term success of any business. Excellent service is a critical means by which any organization can differentiate itself from competition. (Which makes me wonder why more organizations do not focus on this issue.)

Everybody in the organization needs to focus on providing good service, not just frontline customer contact personnel. When such efforts are consistently and constantly led from the top, one is most likely to find a culture of service statesmanship inbred and ingrained at all levels of the organization. One is also likely to find satisfied customers repeating their business.

That combination — excellent service delivery and satisfied repeat customers — is definitely a surefire formula for long-term, sustainable, profitable business growth.

**KEY POINT**: Service Statesmen take an active role in building service excellence into their organizations and constantly reinforce the organization's key service messages and service values to staff, colleagues, and peers.

**TAKING ACTION**: which departments or business units in your organization are known for stellar service delivery? Which are not? How can the learning, ideas, techniques, and culture of the outstanding units be transplanted into other units?

Who are the Service Statesmen in your organization? What do they have in common? How can their passion for outstanding service delivery be leveraged and spread throughout the organization? How can they "infect" their colleagues with their spirit and zeal?

At what level of your organization does the enthusiasm and fanaticism for service delivery seem to come to an end? At what level of the organization is only "lip service" paid to the topic of service excellence? How can the need for organization-wide service statesmanship be communicated to the executives at these levels? (Hint: send them a copy of this week's *Monday Morning Marketing Memo*).

# 20 Service Excellence Management Practices

Customer service — and service quality — are critical managerial topics in business today for many reasons:

- Service quality has strategic importance in the long-term success of the business.

- Excellent customer service is a critical means by which an organization can differentiate itself from competition.

- Everyone in the organization needs to focus on providing good service (not just front-line staff) — from senior managers to customer contact personnel.

**The Best of the Monday Morning Marketing Memo**

As we wrote in *Monday Morning Marketing Memo* #170, inherent in organizations that consistently provide excellent customer service is the very notion of service statesmanship. The two key aspects of service statesmanship are:

- A Service Statesman is a role model, constantly reinforcing the organization's key service messages and service values.

- A Service Statesman is seen by staff as constantly engaged and interested in improving service delivery.

Here are 20 Service Excellence Management Practices that any manager, from a department or business unit manager to the CEO, can and should perform in their role as Service Statesmen:

1. You provide a clear, written statement to employees explaining what you mean by excellent

service and how you will create it for your customers.

2. You make certain that employees can explain their specific role in delivering excellent customer service.

3. You make certain that employees know the day-to-day things they can do to deliver excellent customer service.

4. You communicate to employees on a regular basis about the importance of providing excellent service to customers.

5. You ask employees how customer service quality can be improved.

6. You have your managers set personal examples of good service to customers.

7.  You set standards for response time to customer complaints or questions.

8.  You track the success of your efforts to improve service quality.

9.  You share customers' evaluations of your service quality with all your employees, colleagues, and peers.

10. You reward employees who take a personal interest in resolving customer complaints and problems.

11. You recognize employees who provide superior service to customers.

12. You make it clear that delivering excellent service is important in career advancement decisions.

13.   You keep employees up-to-date on customer expectations.

14.   You encourage employees to go "above and beyond" regular job descriptions for the customer.

15.   You encourage managers to work one-on-one with employees to meet service quality standards.

16.   You train customer contact employees to deal with angry customers.

17.   You provide employees with sufficient training on the company's products and services.

18.   Your policies and procedures are designed to help deliver excellent service.

19.   You define procedures for what to do when mistakes are made or errors are discovered.

20.    You make it easy for customers to reach the right person or business unit when they have problems or questions.

Like most things in business, you have two choices when it comes to being a Service Statesman. You can either talk about it, or you can lead by example via the above 20 practices.

The "talk only" approach, or what might be called the NATO (No Action, Talk Only) approach, is unlikely to produce the desired results.

I always admire the restaurant managers at McDonald's, whom you frequently see with mop and bucket in hand cleaning up after a spill or when customers leave a messy table behind. You know McDonald's is serious about cleanliness when you see the restaurant managers actually doing the cleaning.

The same goes for your business. Customers know exactly how serious your organization is about customer service by observing how your managers act and perform. Likewise, so do your staff.

You can reinforce your dedication and your message about excellent service delivery, to both employees and customers, by putting into practice the 20 managerial habits we have given you this week.

**KEY POINT**: inherent in organizations that consistently provide excellent customer service is the notion of service statesmanship.

**TAKING ACTION**: select four of the 20 managerial practices found in this week's *Monday Morning Marketing Memo* that you would like to start using in your job. For each practice selected, list 3-4 things that you could start doing this week to implement these practices.

Review your policies and procedures. Which ones enable your staff to consistently deliver quality customer service? Which ones hinder them in their pursuit of delivering excellent customer service consistently? How can the latter ones be amended and changed?

Are you seen by your staff as constantly engaged and interested in improving service delivery? What personal steps can you do to improve in this area?

Review your agenda for your last staff meeting. What percentage of the meeting was planned for customer service discussions? For your next 4-5 staff meetings, make sure that customer service is the dominant item on each agenda. Then your staff will know how serious you truly are about this topic.

#### #173

# Message to CEOs:
# Focus on Your Customers!

Here is a scary thought for a Monday morning: many CEOs have lost sight of the importance of customers.

Oh sure, they do know that customers are the folks buying their products and that such sales are important. However, with a focus on quarterly sales and profit figures, head counts, share prices, mergers, cost structures, and other financial ratios, too many corporate leaders have lost the customer insights required to develop and maintain market leadership.

My long-held suspicions on this were confirmed in an article a few months ago in *Inside 1 to 1*, the publication started by the Peppers & Rogers Group. Appropriately titled *"Dear CEO: Don't Leave Customers in the Dust,"* the authors Don Peppers and Martha Rogers write that they are "amazed at the number of CEOs who give interviews on how to grow their companies, or even more fascinating, the CEOs who tell the media how they are going to save their failing companies, and yet make no reference to customers whatsoever."

The authors tracked one month of interviews on business news channel CNBC and report that "23 CEOs discussed their companies' strategies and only six used the word customer" in their responses.

The authors also cite a Deloitte survey in March this year of 50 technology CEOs, which found that only six percent said building customer loyalty is their biggest challenge to sustaining growth. This was well behind other "more important" issues such as bringing new products to market

(27%), hiring salespeople (18%), and developing strategic relationships (15%).

I have noticed this trend for several years in my own reading of business publications. Senior executives are more willing to talk about how they are cutting costs than about the steps their organizations are taking to better understand the changing needs, wants, and desires of customers.

Rare is the executive who claims "we are going to be successful and grow our business because we are listening to our customers and aligning our future products and services with their future needs."

Fortunately, such executives are only rare, not yet extinct.

It is sad to watch stellar organizations go through cycles of poor leadership, wrongly placed focus, and lack of direction simply because senior management decides to take the corporate eyes off customer needs.

**The Best of the Monday Morning Marketing Memo**

This happened to one industry-leading MNC in Southeast Asia, when several changes in management led to cost cuttings, reduction in staffing, and automation replacing humans at key points of interaction with customers. This company was previously the benchmark for customer service in its industry. Today, customers constantly comment that "they used to be the best, but now they are the same as everyone else." Not surprisingly, this company has also seen massive staff turnover within the middle management ranks in the past two years, something that was unheard of only a few years ago.

As the legendary Peter Drucker wrote, "the purpose of business is to attract and keep customers."

This phrase should be posted on the walls nearest every CEO desk.

And next to it should be a poster saying "My primary role as CEO is to ensure we build loyalty with our customers and our employees."

Customers. Employees. Operations. This is what CEOs should focus on, and in the same order as the letters in their titles.

The ones who do this are the ones who will build sustainable and profitable businesses over the long haul.

**KEY POINT**:  senior management should focus on customers first, employees second, and operations third.

**TAKING ACTION**:  review your last dozen public or internal pronouncements on your organization's business strategy. How many of these include comments and directions on customers and customer needs? What priority is given, if any, to customers and customer needs?

Ask yourself, how much time per month do you spend in internal meetings? How much time do you spend attending to operational or financial issues? Then calculate how much time you have remaining for meeting customers and coaching employees. If you are not happy with the results from these calculations, what steps do you need to make immediately to give higher priority to customers and employees?

Go out and meet with customers. Conduct account reviews with your large and high potential customers. Gain insights into their current and future needs. Ask them questions about their business and where their industry is headed. Ask them how they view their relationships with your organization.

Bring together your leadership team for a full-day discussion on customers and customer needs. Enforce this rule: no discussions on sales forecasts, profit projections, cost structures, or internal constraints. Simply discuss your customers' current and future needs. Then discuss how you can profitably provide solutions to these needs.

# Kudos to Qantas

I woke in the pre-dawn hours of last Friday morning to find two text messages on my mobile phone that had come in while I was asleep.

The first was a notice sent at three o'clock that my Singapore to Melbourne flight that evening on Qantas was being postponed from 8pm to around 5am the next morning. The second, also from Qantas, had been sent an hour later informing me of a further delay in departure to 10am. The delays were due to my aircraft not being able to depart Heathrow Airport in London due to the strike activity taking place there on Thursday.

Naturally, as Murphy's Law clearly states, the hotel I staying at was fully booked for that night, so this meant I needed to change hotels for this unplanned additional night in Singapore. To say the least, Friday was starting off on the wrong foot and quickly becoming a day of multiple inconveniences.

By 9:30 I had arranged for another hotel and called the Singapore office of Qantas to check on the latest flight status and to provide them with my local contact details. This is when my state of annoyance turned into one of customer satisfaction.

Answering the phone at the Qantas Singapore sales office was Claire, who promptly took down my details, checked the current status of the flight, and asked me if I need hotel accommodations arranged for the night.

"I've just booked myself at the Grand Hyatt," I replied, explaining that my current hotel was full for the evening.

"In that case, Mr. Howard," she replied, "I will fax the Grand Hyatt and authorize them to bill us directly for your room this evening."

"Wow," I thought, "I hadn't even asked yet whether the airline was going to reimburse me for the hotel bill. Now they have already volunteered to pay for this directly on my behalf. And they haven't asked me to move to a less expensive hotel either."

I thanked her and asked if the airline would try to keep all passengers informed of any future delays or changes in the departure schedule. "We will try our best," she replied, "but it is a very fluid situation right now and we do not know yet when our planes will be able to leave London." She then gave me a priority phone number to call, as well as their local website address, so that I could monitor the situation.

## The Best of the Monday Morning Marketing Memo

When I checked into the Grand Hyatt around 5pm, I was delighted to see that Claire had indeed faxed the hotel and that the proper instructions had been given for the billing of the room charges. I was even more impressed when I found out that the airline had also authorized one dinner and one breakfast to also be charged to them.

About half an hour later Claire called again. I thanked her for the arrangements she had made. "Mr. Howard, I am afraid I have some more bad news," she stated, "your flight has been further delayed now until 7pm on Saturday evening. I will call the hotel and tell them you can also charge your lunch tomorrow to us."

The inconveniences were continuing, but at least Claire and Qantas were doing all they could to minimize my immediate out-of-pocket costs.

On Saturday morning I called the Qantas office to check my flight status. This time one of Claire's colleagues answered my call. After confirming my details, he put me on hold for several minutes. I started to get that empty feeling in the stomach when one instinctively knows further problems are forthcoming.

"Mr. Howard," he said when he came back on line, "your flight has now been delayed until Sunday morning, and even this timing is still tentative." My heart sank. Instead of spending the weekend back home, it now looked like I was destined to send a lonely weekend in Singapore catching up on paperwork and emails.

"However," he continued, "I can move you over to tonight's regularly scheduled flight, which departs at 7:45. May I confirm you on this?"

"Definitely," I replied, starting to smile again. At least I would be home by Sunday morning. And with no more dramas, that is exactly what happened. I actually arrived home in Melbourne before my original flight in London departed Heathrow. And while my inconveniences were not insignificant, they were certainly a whole lot less than the tens of thousands in London and elsewhere whose lives were even more interrupted late last week.

Thinking back on my experiences, from a marketing perspective, Qantas and its people were able to minimize my personal angst and disruptions through:

1) Keeping me informed at all times about the changing flight status.

2) Being proactive in their communications to me, both through personal calls and the use of technology.

3) Using communication technology such as text messages to alert its customers as soon as the problem started to occur.

4) Proactively taking care of customer needs before being asked, such as authorizing my hotel room and meal charges to be billed to them, rather than forcing me into a cumbersome and paper intensive reimbursement claims process.

I am sure the last few days have been very stressful for the Qantas staff around the world as their operations were massively disrupted. But from this customer's experience and perspective, their anguish and the pressures they must have been under were never seen or passed on.

I could have landed in Melbourne yesterday with total anger and disgust at being delayed by 24 hours. Instead, I feel that my needs as a customer were properly, professionally, and personally handled by an organization that projected a caring and concerned attitude about my needs.

And for that, I salute Claire and her colleagues for a situation well handled.

**KEY POINT:** when unexpected problems occur, handle the needs of your customers proactively, professionally, and as personally as possible.

**TAKING ACTION:** review your plans and processes for handling unexpected operational problems. How would you communicate with customers, proactively or only reactively? What steps and processes would be necessary to include proactive customer communications in your plans?

Review your customer databases. Do you capture mobile phone numbers? Have you asked permission from customers to contact them via text messages? Do you have the technology in place to broadcast text messages to customers impacted by a major operational break down? Put a task force together now to review these questions and develop a detailed strategy if necessary.

What would be the key concerns of your customers if you experienced a major operation break down or service disruption? What plans do you have to handle these concerns before asked to do so by customers?

How empowered are your customer contact personnel to handle individual customer needs and solve individual customer problems caused by a major service interruption? Ask your marketing department to investigate these and related questions and, if necessary, to develop procedures and plans that prepare your organization to handle potential service disruptions.

# 20 Quality Customer Service Practices

Two months ago (*Monday Morning Marketing Memo* #170) I wrote about Service Statesmanship, giving the two key aspects of this managerial attribute as:

- A Service Statesman is a role model, constantly reinforcing the organization's key service messages and service values.

- A Service Statesman is seen by staff as constantly engaged and interested in improving service delivery.

I followed this two weeks later in *Monday Morning Marketing Memo* #172 with a list of 20 Service Excellence

Management Practices that each of you can implement, modify, and adapt to lead your business unit or your organization to higher levels of excellent customer service delivery.

And, as you may recall from the most recent *Monday Morning Marketing Memo*, about my experiences with how Qantas handled my 24-hour fight delay, quality customer service has been on my mind quite a bit lately.

Thus, I thought I would share with you 20 Quality Service Practices that any Service Statesman, from a department or business unit manager to the CEO, can and should instill in the individuals within their organization:

1. You make customers aware of the options available, including advantages and disadvantages of each.

2. You respond to customers' needs in a timely and effective way.

3. You keep customers involved as you serve them.

4. You work with customers to completely define their requirements.

5. You are clear with customers around service issues (e.g. costs, results, options).

6. You exhibit flexibility in making whatever adaptations are necessary to enhance working relationships with customers.

7. In proposing solutions to customers, you clearly link the solutions with the customer's business or personal objectives.

8. You are flexible in adapting solutions to customer needs and desires.

9.  You let the customer know exactly what is being done and why.

10. You help customers clarify and prioritize their needs.

11. You keep customers updated on the status of work.

12. You do what is best for the customer, rather than what is best for your own function, when there is a conflict between these two.

13. You encourage customers to give you feedback on your performance.

14. You pay close attention to small details that make a difference to customers.

15. You ask what they expect from you when problems occur.

16. You are committed to providing excellent service.

17.  When a customer experiences a problem, you follow up to see if it has been resolved.

18.  If you cannot help a customer, you are able to refer them to someone else for help.

19.  You will go out of your way to solve a customer need or problem that is out of the ordinary or that requires extra effort.

20.  You will treat your colleagues and peers as internal customers worthy of the same respect, treatment, and concern as you would give to external customers.

In reviewing how Qantas handled my personal situation 10 days ago, I can spot how several of the above practices were put into action (particularly numbers 6, 8, 9, and 14).

Outstanding customer service appears to be ingrained in numerous organizations, and woefully lacking in others. Those who get this right are the ones who have no trouble keeping good customers and getting these to return time and time again.

Those who do not implement these 20 Quality Service Practices in a consistent manner are the ones with high customer attrition rates and high employee turnover levels.

If you want to be a true Service Statesman in your organization, you can lead by example and reinforce the importance of constantly improving service delivery by inculcating these 20 Quality Service Practices into your business unit.

**KEY POINT**: outstanding customer service delivery is ingrained in organizations that implement the 20 Quality Service Practices in a consistent manner.

**TAKING ACTION**: select four of the 20 practices found in this week's *Monday Morning Marketing Memo* that you would like your organization to start using. For each practice selected, list 3-4 things that you could start doing this week to implement these practices.

Review your policies and procedures. Which ones enable your staff to consistently deliver quality customer service? Which ones hinder them in pursuit of delivering excellent customer service consistently? How can the latter ones be amended and changed?

Review your agenda for your last staff meeting. What percentage of the meeting was planned for customer service discussions? For your next 4-5 staff meetings, make sure that customer service is the dominant item on each agenda. Then your staff will know how serious you truly are about this topic.

#179

# Points of Interaction:
# Gaining a Competitive Edge

A critical aspect of customer retention are the key touch points where customers see, hear, feel, taste, touch, and experience your products, services, people, environment, processes, procedures, policies, and attitudes.

This is extremely true in many of today's markets, where intense competition and commodity functions and features of competing product offers lead to price-driven and promotion-driven marketing tactics.

As I wrote in *Monday Morning Marketing Memo* #157 at the start of this year, the experiences customers receive through their interactions with your organization will make or break your ability to develop a long-term relationship with them. The experiences customers receive will also impact your immediate sales and short-term relationships, as well as any hope you have of turning casual customers into loyal ones.

Competitive advantages are eroding faster than ever in today's world.

Great products, top-notch technologies, and superb customer service are merely the cost of entry into today's markets. How do you get a sustainable edge when all of these supposedly competitive advantages are easily replicated?

One route to a sustainable competitive edge is how your organization interacts with customers.

According to the authors of the article *Beyond Better Products: Capturing Value in Customer Interactions* (MIT Sloan Management Review), "customers often value how they interact with their suppliers as much or more than what they actually buy." Their conclusions were based on data collected from more than 1,500 senior executives in interviews and discussion groups on the topic "why do your customers choose to buy from you rather than your competitors?"

I believe the authors are correct, especially when it comes to services and non-tangible purchases (creative services from an agency, legal advice from a law firm, recommendations and therapies from a health care provider, etc.).

Taking this further, authors Jeffrey F. Rayport and Bernard J. Jaworski argue in their book *Best Face Forward: Why Companies Must Improve Their Service Interfaces With Customers* that overwhelmingly intense competition and markets where products and services become commodities overnight have combined to make superior interface capabilities the only lasting competitive advantage.

According to them, companies must create more effective (yield a better quality customer interaction) and more efficient (incent a better interaction at a lower cost per interaction) interfaces with customers to create and sustain true competitive advantages. Other than their overuse of the word interfaces (I much prefer interactions, as it is more consumer friendly and less of a technical lingo), these authors are on the right track.

If you are interested in learning more about their views, there is an excellent CMO Magazine audio interview with former Harvard Business School Professor Rayport. It is well worth listening to this 30-minute interview as Rayport explores why the points of interactions that determine how customers view a company has become the new frontier of competitive advantage.

At the end of the day, the customer experiences at every point of interaction with your organization create the brand experience. To keep customers returning, these unique brand experiences must be customer-focused and virtually imitation proof.

Doing so not only creates a unique corporate brand that cannot be copied, but simultaneously creates strong emotional and rational reasons for your good customers to continuing doing business with you.

Your points of interaction with customers may be the only competitive advantage you have. They may also be your weakest points. The old proverb about a chain being only as strong as its weakest link applies readily to the strength of your customer relationships and the points of interaction upon which these relationships are built.

The bottom line is: if you are not delivering the right kinds of customer experiences at *every* point of interaction, all your other relationship building efforts will be for naught.

**KEY POINT:** one route to a sustainable competitive edge is how your organization interacts with customers.

**TAKING ACTION:** have your senior managers brainstorm and develop a list of answers to the question "why are your customers buying from you and not from your competitors?" Analyze these responses in terms of product features/functions and *the ways customers interact with your organization.*

Which of your customer interfaces are machine driven? Which are people driven? Which are a combination of the two? Survey your key customers to ascertain if these interfaces are delivering the quality of interactions they want and, if not, how would they like to see changes made?

Give us a call or an email to discuss your customer interactions strategy. We can help you analyze your needs and work with you to create better interactions that cannot be copied or replicated. You may also benefit from our two-day workshop on *Innovative Strategies for Reaching (and Keeping) Good Customers* or from our half-day interactive program *Customer Retention: Creating Value for Customers in the Service Sector.*

**#183**

# 12 Marketing Philosophies

Now that I have started drafting my own personal and professional New Year's Resolutions, I thought I would share with you 12 of my personal marketing philosophies that will enable each *Monday Morning Marketing Memo* reader to develop his or her own set of resolutions and goals.

In no particular order of importance, these 12 marketing philosophies are:

1. Segment customers based on customer needs, not the needs of your organization and not based around the structures of your existing organizational chart.

2. In order for customers to see you as a unique brand or service provider, you need to treat them as unique

individuals — with individually unique needs, wants, desires, likes, and dislikes.

3.  Remember that when dealing with customers (even in the B2B world) you are dealing with fellow human beings, not revenue streams. Thus, every customer matters and every customer interaction matters (especially to the customer).

4.  The era of mass production required mass communications. Today's era of individual customers and smaller customer segments requires a more individualized approach to marketing communications.

5.  Your fellow employees communicate your brand's true value to customers. Every employee interaction with a customer or prospect, therefore, either

enhances or denigrates your brand reputation and the customer's brand experience.

6. With the increased importance of Corporate Social Responsibility, your corporate image is more important than ever. How your corporate image is managed is critical. After all, competitors can replicate your products and services, beat you up on price, outspend you in promotions, and outperform you in distribution. However, the one thing competitors cannot copy or duplicate is a well defined, well managed corporate image.

7. The Four Ps of Customer Retention (People, Policies, Processes / Procedures, and Prevention) are more relevant for retaining customers captured through the time honored marketing mix than the original Four Ps of marketing (product, price, promotion, and place) created over 40 years ago by Professor Philip Kotler.

8.  It is not what you communicate, it is what your customers hear that is most important. Customers have learned how to filter out traditional marketing messages and now, with devices such as TiVo and email filters, have the tools to do so. Getting customers to hear your marketing messages requires greater creativity, increased innovation, and heightened integration.

9.  Profitability is not very useful or informative for understanding customer needs.

10. Focus on your customers and their needs, wants, desires, likes, and dislikes. Remember, if you don't take care of your customers, someone else will.

11. CRM works better when it means Customer Retention Marketing. Customer Retention is the *art of keeping*

*good customers*™ and should be the cornerstone foundation for all long-term marketing strategies.

12.    *If it touches the customer, it's a marketing issue.*™ Marketing is the integrator across all business lines and all internal departments.

I hope you are able to put some, if not all, of the above marketing philosophies into practice.


**KEY POINT**:  if it touches the customer, it's a marketing issue.™

**TAKING ACTION**: what are your own personal marketing philosophies? How do these impact the short-term and long-term decisions you make?

Circulate the list above to your staff or fellow colleagues. Discuss which ones instinctively feel right for your organization. Why?

How could these be disseminated widely throughout your department, business unit, or entire organization?

**#189**

# A World of Customer Experiences

Customers buy experiences.

That is the premise behind the book *Building Great Customer Experiences* which I had the pleasure of reading last month.

The authors, Colin Shaw and John Ivens, have seven philosophies for building a great customer experience, including:

- Great customer experiences are a source of long-term competitive advantage.

- Great customer experiences are both revenue generating and cost reducing.

- Great customer experiences are an embodiment of the brand.

In a world of product parity and commoditization of both products and services, their arguments make a great deal of sense.

It is interesting to observe how many organizations focus only on the customer experience at the beginning of the sales cycle, rather than at all points of interaction.

For instance, how many large retail stores have a greeter who welcomes people as they enter the store, but have no one to say "thank you" as the customers leave with their purchases?

Even worse, there are the stores that have people at the exits checking everyone's shopping bags to make sure nothing is being stolen. How many thieves are caught or prevented by this? A few a week? That is not necessarily a good trade-off for making hundreds of people a day feel like their privacy is being violated or, worse, that they are being falsely considered as shoplifters.

People often cite the phrase that first impressions matter most. From a marketing perspective, I disagree. I often write that it is the last impression that matters most.

For instance, you may have a wonderful check-in experience and an enjoyable in-flight experience, but if your bags are not on the carousel promptly (or at all) at your final destination that will be the thing you remember most about your flight and the airline you flew.

Or, you may have wonderful help in the aisles of a store, but if you encounter a rude and surly cashier at the check-out counter that will be what you remember most of that particular visit to that store.

# The Best of the Monday Morning Marketing Memo

The entire shopping experience at Amazon is a delightful experience. This company understands the mentality of people who want to buy books, videos, CDs, and other merchandise from an online outlet. Likewise, Borders understands the mentality of people who want to buy books, videos, CDs, and other merchandise in a "bricks and mortar" retail outlet. Both are sellers of books. But, more important, both are sellers (and deliverers) of unique customer experiences.

The success of Starbucks comes not just from the taste of their coffee, but from the customer experiences they deliver to their sit-down and chat, take-away, and even drive-through customers. Buying and drinking a coffee from Starbucks is an experience, one that an increasing number of customers around the world appear to enjoy and repeat.

One of the secrets to increasing customer loyalty is to fully understand all the experiences customers have with your organization when they investigate, evaluate, purchase, use, and dispose of your products and services. Each point of interaction is an opportunity to build long-term customer loyalty. Each point of interaction is an opportunity for your organization to better understand your customers.

Your competitors can copy your products, replicate your services, and match your pricing strategies.

This means that the customer experience you deliver is one of the few marketing advantages remaining to keep your customers loyal and to convert occasional buyers into long-term and loyal customers.

In a world of customer experiences, sustainable growth will come to those who monitor and improve the experiences of customers at each and every point of interaction.

**KEY POINT**: every point of interaction is an opportunity to build long-term customer loyalty.

**TAKING ACTION**: walk through every location that your customers visit or see. What needs cleaning, fixing, brightening, toning down? Who are the staff talking with: themselves or customers? What do customers see in your environment — a company in control or one so cluttered it appears to be in control of nothing?

Touch everything your customers will touch. What feels good? What does not? What is warm? What is cold? Is it nice to feel? How do you react to this? How do your customers react to this?

Close your eyes and listen to the environment. What do you hear? Is the music too loud or not appropriate for your target customers? Are the staff talking about themselves or about customers and their needs?

Examine all forms. Fill them out as if you were a customer. How can these be improved?

Call your call center with a complaint. How is this handled?

Call your call center with a query. How is this handled?

Review your website. How easy is it to contact your organization via the website? What information is lacking or missing (from a customer's perspective)?

#190

# The Customer Experience
# Is More Important Than Price

From a customer's perspective, every interaction with your organization is a customer experience. And each of these interactions has a cost to the customer — in terms of money, time, or both.

If these experiences are consistently good, customers are more likely to repeat business with you; giving you the kind of customer loyalty your organization truly desires.

A recent research study from Amdocs, a leading provider of software and services that enable integrated customer management, supports the importance of the customer experience on customer retention.

# The Best of the Monday Morning Marketing Memo

Called the Customer Experience Survey, the survey reveals that consumers and businesses around the world say that they are more likely to stick with a telecom provider based on the quality of the customer experience than on the cost of its service. For an industry that seems driven by constant cost pressures and incessant price cutting, this survey may be quite an eye opener.

For those of you who hate being put on hold when calling a customer contact center, you will not be surprised to learn that 57% of the respondents to this survey said they would pay extra not to be put on hold, or have to talk with multiple service representatives, when dealing with a call center.

This survey queried over 1,000 consumers and 400 businesses in the United States and the United Kingdom about their interactions with telecom providers. While the results are industry specific, I believe similar findings would occur in most other industries and markets across the globe.

After all, the frustrations that customers feel about the service they receive, particularly when trying to reach a frontline support person, are universal.

"The Amdocs Customer Experience Survey proves that keeping customers happy is not just about reducing prices," says Mr. Michael Matthews, Chief Marketing Officer of Amdocs. "By adopting an integrated customer management strategy, providers can get a full picture of their customer interactions. From there, they can identify customer needs and provide a differentiated and intentional customer experience. That is the right strategy regardless of whether the customers are consumers or large corporations."

Customers buy experiences.

Customers pay for the experiences they receive from your organization — either in money, time, or both.

For many customers, perhaps even a majority, time is a more valuable currency than money.

As a result, many customers are willing to pay for convenience. In the Amdocs survey, a majority of respondents claimed they were willing to pay an extra US$5 a month if it meant that they would not be put on hold and not have to talk to multiple service representatives when contacting a telecom call center.

In a world of product parity and commoditization of both products and services, it may seem like price is the most important determining factor in the customer buying decision-making process.

But as the Amdocs survey results show, this may not always be the case. Even in the highly competitive telecoms industry, where product parity and service commoditization are the status quo, there are market segments eagerly willing to make purchase decisions on factors other than price.

In a world of customer experiences, sustainable growth will come to those who monitor and improve the experiences of customers at each and every point of interaction.

After all, good customers place a higher value on their experiences in dealing with organizations over the prices paid for products and services.

And since customer retention is all about *the art of keeping good customers,*™ focusing your efforts on improving convenience to customers and reducing their time costs when dealing with your organization is one of the best ways to improve the overall experiences of your customers.

**KEY POINT**: customers pay for the experiences they receive from your organization — either in money, time, or both.

**TAKING ACTION**: survey the top 20% of your customers and ask them specifically what steps you could take to improve your convenience to them. Also be sure to ask them if they would be willing to pay a fee to receive improved and more convenient service.

Monitor your call abandon rates, as well as the length of time customers spend on hold, at all your telephone service centers. Survey your customers about their experiences with your phone and call centers. Where is improvement needed?

Benchmark your customer experiences with those of your competitors. How can you make the customer experience a point of differentiation so that you do not need to compete as much on price?

**#197**

# Customer ENTHUSIASM

While doing research over the weekend for my next book, I came across a note I had written to myself many months ago on creating enthusiasm for customers within an organization.

In the note, I turned the word enthusiasm into an acronym:

**Enjoy** your work. When you enjoy your work, customers enjoy you.

**Never** say "no." Find ways to say "yes" to customers.

**Take** the time needed to fully satisfy the customer. The best gift to offer customers is your attention and time.

**Hustle**. Time is valuable, help customers save it by serving them efficiently and fast.

**Understand** before trying to be understood. You cannot satisfy customer needs until you listen.

**Smile**. Your smile tells the customer he or she has come to the right person.

**Insist** on astonishing. Merely satisfying customers is not enough. Astonish.

**Ask** if the customer is completely satisfied. Ensure customer satisfaction by asking if there is anything else you can do and if what you have done is enough to have them return to you again in the future.

**Suggestive** sell. Suggest related items that make the customer's purchase better.

**Meaningful** "thank you." A sincere thank you builds loyalty that brings back customers.

Legendary American football coach Vince Lombardi is quoted as saying "If you aren't fired with enthusiasm, you will be fired with enthusiasm."

We are not suggesting that you need to start enthusiastically firing your staff. But we do hope that the ENTHUSIASM acronym might be useful to you in firing up the enthusiasm of your staff for your customers.

Otherwise, it may be your customers who fire you with enthusiasm.

**KEY POINT**:  never say "no" to a customer; find ways of saying "yes" instead.

**TAKING ACTION**: are your frontline staff and customer contact personnel only measured on quantitative scores such as how many customers per work shift they handle? Why?

How can you institute some qualitative scoring measures tracking how their handling of customers impacts your customer retention results?

Train your staff to take the time necessary to fully understand the needs, wants, desires, likes, and dislikes of your customers. Time spent with customers is rarely wasted.

Teach your staff not to be afraid to ask customers if they are fully satisfied. Without asking, you will never know their true feelings. Asking shows that the organization cares and wants these customers to return again and again.

#200

# If it touches the customer, it's a marketing issue™

Many years ago I developed a personal marketing philosophy that I believe forms the core principle of marketing — *if it touches the customer, it's a marketing issue.*™

By focusing my thinking on what touches the customer, and how these impact and influence customers' purchase decisions, I became highly adept at developing marketing and positioning strategies, first for my employers and then for my clients upon creating Howard Marketing Services in 1993.

Of course, everything your organization does touches your customers. This is why I advocate that long-term, sustainable success requires a customer-centric, marketing-led approach. The key here is being customer focused, not just marketing led. Success will not automatically result from the traditional implementation of marketing techniques such as brand advertising, one-way communications with customers, lack of awareness of customer experiences, and reactive customer service strategies.

Rather, sustainable growth and success, as well as long-term customer loyalty, results from combining and modifying those traditional marketing approaches with TLC (think like customers), proactive customer engagements that lead to long-term customer satisfaction, two-way communications at all customer points of interaction, and a focus on understanding and learning from customer experiences with your products and services.

Prolonged success also results from adapting your current organizational processes and practices to better align yourself with the changing values of customers.

One of those changing customer values is choices and flexibility. Customers want both choices and flexibility, particularly when deciding what products and services will provide solutions to their needs, wants, and desires. Of course, when it comes to the actual purchase and use of a product or service, it is a bit different. As B. Joseph Pine points out in the book *Mass Customization,* "Customers don't want choice. They just want exactly what they want."

Only an organization that is fully focused on identifying the needs, wants, and desires of its customers will be able to provide exactly what they want. Then, if you give customers a little bit more than they expect, you are well on your way to developing long-term customer loyalty. As Susan Lyne, CEO of Martha Stewart Living Omnimedia said, "If people get what they expect from a brand — and more — they're going to stick with it."

Product Marketing. Brand Managers. Product Managers. Organization structures based on product lines or product groups. This is where the traditional focus of marketing has been, and unfortunately still remains — on products.

But, as I have often stated: "A product is or a service is just your point of entry. A loyal customer is the true goal."

Having loyal customers should be the goal of every organization. The purpose of business, as the legendary Peter Drucker wrote, is "to create a customer." In my view, the ultimate role of marketing is **to create and keep good customers, to the benefit of customers, the organization, and other stakeholders**.

Business is not just about sales, contracts, cash flow, internal rates of return, ROI, and profitability. Even Henry

Ford recognized this when he said, "a business that makes nothing but money is a poor kind of business."

Using traditional marketing techniques, being "customer oriented" has meant operating in order to meet the needs of the typical customer, or the average customer. Businesses today cannot afford to focus on the average customer. Your future growth, and future profitability, comes from satisfying the needs of your most valuable customers.

To treat your most valuable customers as your most valued customers requires that they be treated as individuals — with individual needs, wants, desires, likes, and dislikes.

To treat valuable customers as individuals requires the understanding that anything that touches these customers is a marketing concern. It also means understanding that everything you do as an organization — and sometimes the things that you do not do — touches your customers.

The bottom line is simply this: **if it touches the customer, it's a marketing issue™**.

This simple phrase births an entire marketing philosophy that you can use to develop sustainable growth and a loyal customer base for your own products and services.

It means doing things — particularly "marketing" — differently than you are doing them today. It means putting the needs of your customers first, before those of the organization. It means inculcating the skills of thinking from the customer's perspective throughout the organization. And it means delivering your brand through customer experiences rather than paid advertising.

It will feel different, doing all these things, of that I can assure you. But I can also assure you so too will be the results.

**KEY POINT**:  if it touches the customer, it's a marketing issue.™

**TAKING ACTION**:  what is the main focus of your internal meetings? Products or customers? Sales results or customer needs? How can you spend more time discussing customers and their needs and less time discussing other matters?

How do you reward those in the organization that exhibit high levels of customer intensity? How do you publicize their efforts internally? What can be done to improve these areas and turn your customer-focused folks into internal heroes?

What is your marketing strategy based on — products or customers? Are your marketing plans based on product groupings and goals or customers and customer segments? Now is the time to change from product-driven strategies to customer-driven ones.

**#202**

# Customer Churn Continues Unabated

Customer attrition rates remain unbelievably high, despite (or maybe because of) continued investments by corporations in CRM technology.

According to a study of 1,000 consumers by Accenture, 18% of respondents reported they stopped conducting business with at least one retailer within the past year due to poor service. A significant proportion of consumers in this survey also stopped doing business during the previous 12 months with Internet Service Providers (15%), banks (14%), telephone companies (12%), wireless/cell phone companies (11%), and cable/satellite TV service providers (10%).

That's a whole lot of customer churn going on.

It is little wonder that Larry Weber, founder of the Weber Shandwick public relations firm, says that "most customers are nomads."

When viewed in the light of another piece of research, perhaps these findings are not so surprising after all. A destinationCRM.com reader poll conducted in October last year reports that:

a) 39% of customer contact centers do not measure either customer loyalty or customer satisfaction.

b) 19% measure only customer satisfaction.

c) 42% measure both customer loyalty and customer satisfaction.

This means that a full 58% of customer contact centers do not measure customer loyalty at all, at least according to this reader poll.

If you are not measuring customer loyalty, then you probably have little idea how to manage and reduce customer attrition.

Building a sustainable and profitable business requires a customer strategy that is centered on creating (and measuring) customer loyalty.

Doing so requires keen customer insight, not million dollar CRM computer systems. In most cases, the thousands and millions of dollars spent on CRM hardware would have been better spent on hiring, training, motivating, and retaining good staff who have your customers' needs, wants, desires, and best interests in mind at all times.

In another Accenture research study reported in the article *Meeting Individual Customer Expectations* by Michael Breault, "delivering consistently on the brand promise plays a greater role in creating loyal customers than any other customer-facing capability does." In fact, according to the study, "regardless of their industry or business model (B2C, B2B, etc.), developing and delivering a branded customer experience comprises 33% of a company's ability to achieve strong customer loyalty."

In his article, Breault also cites a Bain & Company study that found some 80% of companies believed they are delivering a "superior experience" to their customers, while the customers of these firms rated only 8% of them as truly delivering a superior customer experience. Now that is a perception gap!

It is a perception gap that is caused by the corporate focus on using transactional data to define the relationships with customers and a lack of insight on customer attitudes, behaviors, and perceptions. It is also caused by the reliance on demographic segmentation instead of segmentation based on customer needs.

It is also caused by companies not listening to their customers. A study by customer experience research and consulting firm Strativity Group concludes that too many companies do not properly use the information garnered from customer surveys. The two biggest problems cited in this study were:

a) although a majority of the respondents (59%) claimed to design customer surveys with strategic intentions, only a small minority (23%) managed to obtain internal buy-in for change in response to customer survey results.

b) only 45% of the 200+ plus firms surveyed around the world could translate their customer survey results into actions.

One of the other problems identified in the Strativity Group survey is that 69% of the survey participants reported that they faced internal struggles with people arguing about the validity of the customer survey results. As the report concludes, "the study results indicate only a superficial and incremental commitment on the part of companies to their customer studies and to acting upon customer insight."

When these various independent research studies are reviewed in aggregate, one reaches the conclusion that:

a) Customer attrition rates of 10% to 15% per annum are likely to remain for years to come.

b) Until companies start to measure customer loyalty, they will remain ignorant and naive about this critical bottom-line impacting issue.

c) Too many companies are fooling themselves (or their senior management, but not their customers) by conducting customer surveys that do not result in action and customer experience enhancing changes.

One of these days, corporations are going to understand the cost of customer attrition. At least that is my hope.

Until then, of course, any company that makes customer insight and customer loyalty a focal point of their business operations will have a significant advantage in creating long-term, sustainable growth and profitability.

**KEY POINT**: if you are not measuring customer loyalty, then you probably have little idea how to manage and reduce customer attrition.

**TAKING ACTION**: review the results of your two most recent customer surveys and then identify what actions were taken as a result of the surveys. Was sufficient action taken? Why or why not? What actions were overlooked or not implemented? Why?

What is your customer attrition rate? If you do not know, how can you start monitoring this immediately? Your customer attrition rate should be a critical component of your Marketing Dashboard. Is it?

How can you start to measure customer loyalty? Make measuring customer loyalty one of your top goals for the coming year.

**#207**

# Terrible Marketing Advice

A few weeks ago I downloaded some product information from a company selling CRM software.

About a week later I received an extremely delightful email that said in part:

> *Recently, you requested information about "XYZ CRM". I want to thank you for your interest in our product, which is why I'm going to send you a valuable marketing course that will help you evaluate your current marketing efforts and give you tips that will definitely increase your profits.*
>
> *This marketing course is called "6 Magnetic Marketing Secrets To Explode Your Profits." You'll*

*get an email once a week that gives you powerful marketing advice for your business, which you can use right away to close more sales and make more money with your business.*

I was suitably impressed...until I received part one of their six-part so-called "marketing" course.

Called "*Secret #1: The Real Definition of Successful Marketing*," this initial communiqué states that "there are only three factors that influence the profitability of any marketing effort. The smartest marketing minds on the planet have sifted these factors down to this simple, but powerful formula:

The Right Message. To the Right Market. At the Right Time!

That is the problem when someone tries to boil marketing down to a "simple formula." They tend to ignore factors like having the right product solution, the right distribution and delivery system, the right branding strategy and, of course, a profitable pricing strategy.

Of course, these guys are trying to sell CRM software solutions, so they appear only concerned with the "selling side" of the marketing equation. But nevertheless, that does not give them to right to broadcast such a misleading interpretation of the essence of marketing to their potential customers.

If they wanted to use an all-encompassing phrase to depict the real meaning and quintessence of marketing, they should have asked to use the one created by the mind of this marketing professional:

*If it touches the customer, it's a marketing issue*™

Now, with their focus on selling CRM systems, and their pitch on tracking all customer and prospect communications, these guys compound the error of their ways by offering free marketing advice in this so-called "marketing course."

They claim that "not using the three marketing success factors and/or little or no direct response offers costs companies millions in missed sales every year!"

That is almost funny, because from almost all the articles I have read about the problems of implementing CRM systems, it appears that it is these implementation problems that are costing companies hundreds of millions in missed sales and lost customers every year.

But that is beside the point, at least for now.

What galls me the most about their free marketing advice is their first point on how to "fix" the problems of these lost sales. This advice is to:

*Never waste money on image advertising, or at least keep it to a minimum and only try creating yourself or your company as a brand after becoming profitable!*

What utter nonsense! What utter lack of understanding of how to create and leverage a brand. What total confusion and wrong impression about the strategic importance of having a strong corporate brand in today's ultra-competitive markets.

In other words, what total idiots!

It is only a sense of professionalism, combined with pity for their misguided ways, which prevents my total outrage at their spreading their mistaken and erroneous claptrap from telling our *Monday Morning Marketing Memo* readers who "XYZ CRM" actually is.

I will share this week's *Monday Morning Marketing Memo* with the person sending out their email campaign. I will also point them to the classic advertisement from McGraw-Hill that ran in the 1950. The copy platform of this ad was quite simple, yet effective:

I don't know who you are.

I don't know your company.

I don't know what your company stands for.

I don't know your company's customers.

I don't know your company's record.

I don't know your company's reputation.

Now — what is it you wanted to sell me?

Come to think of it, in terms of the "XYZ CRM" company, I don't know who they are, what they stand for, their customers, their track record, or even their reputation. All I know is that they give out awful free marketing advice.

And for me, that's enough NOT to recommend them to anyone now, or in the near future.

Perhaps they ought to reconsider their own policies, and their own advice, by figuring out how to create a strong corporate brand for themselves that can be leveraged for greater sales, higher margins, and better profitability.

In the meantime, I caution all readers to be leery of free marketing advice, especially when this is promulgated by sales people more interested in meeting quarterly sales targets than in helping you to better understand how to use the power of marketing to create and grow your own sustainable business.

**KEY POINT**: do not overlook the strategic importance of having a strong corporate brand in today's ultra-competitive markets.

**TAKING ACTION**: be leery of free marketing advice, particularly when it is not proffered by professional marketing people, but by those eager to sell you their goods and services.

When was the last time you took a good, hard look at your corporate brand and the impact of this on both your future sales and your customer retention levels? Have you become so comfortable with your corporate brand that you have forgotten to check its pulse with your customers, prospects, employees, and the communities you serve?

Contact us today for an in-depth discussion on how we can help you evaluate your corporate brand and devise strategies to leverage your corporate image to enhance the sustainable growth of your business.

**#208**

# Green Marketing Is Here To Stay

Back in August 2000, in *Monday Morning Marketing Memo #34*, I wrote that "environmental impact" was one of the seven key areas where customers were more likely to focus their value judgments in the future.

Little did I know in 2000 when I wrote these words that this "core constituency" I was referring to would evolve from a small, but significant, silent minority to an overwhelming plurality of vocal customers.

Now, many years later, "green marketing" is on the cusp of becoming a critical aspect and focal point in marketing. This, however, will not be some fashionable, short-term trend that burns brightly for a couple of years and quickly dies away.

In our book *Powerful Marketing Minutes: 50 Ways to Develop Market Leadership in the 21st Century*, we elaborated on how we saw companies and organizations being able to benefit from the high value that some customers would place on support for the environment and environmental issues.

Research today confirms that a growing multitude customers are placing a higher value on environmental impact in their own personal and business-related purchasing decision-making processes.

As a result, the environmental movement is one area that organizations seem keen to associate with these days. However, environmentally conscious consumers are well aware that, except for a handful of truly exceptional cases, most of these efforts are tactical promotions and many are more self-serving than environmentally serving.

However, for companies that do want to truly benefit from the environmental movement, there will be a core constituency available who will highly value the use of environmentally friendly materials and processes in the manufacturing and distribution of products.

These opportunities run the gamut from the use of recycled raw materials to incorporating materials, parts, ingredients, and packaging that are biodegradable into your final products.

For example, research earlier this year from Cone, the Boston-based cause-related marketing agency, revealed that customers in the USA are looking to companies to act on today's environmental concerns. According to their research, a full 93% of Americans believe companies have a responsibility to help preserve the environment.

"Companies ultimately need to engage consumers and effectively communicate the impact their business practices and products have on the environment," the agency says. "Consumers are listening."

The survey also found that 32% of Americans say they are more interested in environmental issues than they were a year ago, and this is directly impacting their purchasing decisions. For example, 85% of those surveyed said they would consider switching products or services if they learned about a company's negative corporate responsibility practices. Additionally, 47% say they have actually purchased environmentally friendly goods or services in the last year. (About 93% say they are conserving energy, and 89% are recycling.)

Self-interest, of course, is still the biggest motivator in consumer purchase decisions, with saving money and improving health two of the largest motivating factors. Hence, it is not surprising that 72% of the respondents in this survey also said they would be willing to pay more for an environmentally sound purchase if it saves them money in the long run. This helps to explain why products like the Toyota Prius and long-lasting light bulbs are so hot in the USA. Likewise, 58% also said they would be willing to pay more for products that also provide a health advantage.

According to the article I read, the agency thinks that as consumers expand their decision making framework, being green will not be enough. "With retailers like Wal-Mart, Home Depot and Marks & Spencer offering more earth-friendly choices across many product lines, consumers can more easily make those sorts of decisions," says Mindy Gomes Casseres, account director at Cone.

The article also says that consumers are "becoming increasing adept at focusing on how key issues change from industry to industry, she says, in large part due to advertising initiatives like Starbucks' explanations about fair trade."

"Right now, we suspect a lot of consumer awareness centers on conversations about climate change," she says, "but that doesn't mean consumers don't have things like human rights in mind when they go shopping for footwear or apparel."

Green "has gone mainstream," says Allen Adamson, managing director at branding agency Landor Associates and author of *BrandSimple* in an article in USA Today last April. "Everyone has jumped on this bandwagon." He cites the popularity of Al Gore's global-warming documentary, *An Inconvenient Truth*, along with an increased emphasis on climate issues in schools, as two huge factors fueling consumer interest in the green movement.

As we wrote in *Powerful Marketing Minutes* many years ago, "if there is an opportunity for your organization to be truly involved and supportive of the environment, not only will we all benefit (from cleaner air, reduced use of fossil fuels, etc.), but you are likely to develop a core nucleus of dedicated and loyal customers.

Let's see: helping the environment while simultaneously creating a loyal and dedicated customer base. That is a business model for all of us to consider.

**KEY POINT**: a growing multitude of your customers are undoubtedly placing a higher value on environmental impact in their own personal and business-related purchasing decisions.

**TAKING ACTION**: what role does green marketing play in your marketing plans? How can you truly help the environment and, at the same time, capitalize on your involvement?

Is there an affinity group of environmentally conscious customers who would appreciate and reward your organization for deeper involvement and/or conspicuous concern for the environment?

What have you got to lose by being concerned about the environment? What have you got to gain?

**#213**

# Being Customer Focused Means Being Easy To Do Business With

Larry Weber, the founder of public relations firm Weber Shandwick , says that "most customers are nomads."

And rightfully so. Too few companies and organizations deserve customer loyalty.

The reasons why customers are nomads are numerous:

- Service delivery is inconsistent.

- Customer service is perfunctory and uncaring, lacking warmth or even pleasantness.

- There is no recognition of the customer's previous engagements and interactions with the organization.

- There is a lack of personalization to meet individual needs, wants, desires, likes, or dislikes.

- "Value-added" pricing and packaging comes without the value add.

- Customer rewards programs are thought to be true customer loyalty programs.

Despite all these hurdles, customers do want to be loyal!

After all, loyalty saves the customer time (our most precious commodity in today's world). Plus consistent service delivery can be anticipated, expected, and planned for. No surprises results in the customer not having to make new plans or contemplate new decisions.

How can you obtain customer loyalty? Does becoming customer focused work? What does it mean to be customer focused anyway?

Call it customer focused, customer centric, customer caring, or any other clever phrase you want. Being customer focused may boil down to one simple question — are you easy to do business with?

How do you rate in terms of convenience, easy ordering, customizable products and services, personalized delivery terms, and flexible terms and conditions?

Being easy to do business with is more about pre-sales and post-sales support than about the core features of your products or services.

For example, I buy almost all my books from Internet retailer Amazon. Unlike the big chain bookstores, or even my local neighborhood book store, Amazon is easy to do business with because:

- The titles I want are always in stock.

- I never have waste time while the checkout person chats idly with the customer in front of me.

- I never have to search for a knowledgeable staff member to help me find out where the book I'm looking for has been placed.

- I do not consume fuel driving to Amazon, nor do I have to wait or pay for a parking space.

- The time and petrol costs I save more than outweigh and off-set any shipping charges I pay.

- My personal shipping addresses and credit card details (yes, both are plural for a reason, another sign of their flexibility and customization) are on file, so I easily check out with the mere click of a few buttons.

- Amazon notifies me when my order has been shipped, saving me the time to follow up.

- Amazon gives me an approximate delivery date, thus setting my expectations (which they then always meet).

- Even when I place an order on Saturday it gets shipped the next day — a Sunday!

I cannot think of a single thing Amazon could do to make it easier to do business with them. I have read where Amazon founder and CEO Jeff Bezos is passionate about improving the customer experience. For me, he is certainly hitting all the right buttons.

Amazon is a great example of a company that is practicing Customer Retention Marketing by being easy to do business with. As a result, they are keeping good customers (like me) loyal in terms of both buying behavior and brand preference.

Customers do not need (or want) to be nomads. All it takes to change this is being easy to do business with.

**KEY POINT**: being customer focused may boil down to one simple question — are you easy to do business with?

**TAKING ACTION**: ask yourself, is your organization easy to do business with? What rules, procedures, and processes do you have that make it hard for your customers to do business with you?

How could you make it easier for customers to do business with you? What changes can you make in the areas of convenience, order placement, product or service customization, delivery, and other terms and conditions that would make it easier for customers to do business with you?

Review with your major customers which of your processes, policies, procedures, terms, conditions, and other elements drive them crazy and make them wish you did things differently.

**#218**

# Entering the Era of Responsibility.

# Authenticity Required.

We live in a world today where the trust levels for businesses, corporations, governments, politicians, business leaders, and just about every other formal institution at or near all-time lows.

Refresh your mind with some of the headlines and key stories of recent years: financial institutions going bankrupt, Toyota mishandling a global recall of vehicles, the BP oil spill in the Gulf of Mexico; trust in politicians around the globe going down the drain, brand endorsing sports stars caught cheating on their spouses – impacting not only their personal lives but the employees and corporations associated with their endorsed brands.

Fortunately, in the world of marketing, as in science, for every action there is almost always an equal and opposite reaction.

I have been observing media trends, researching numerous topics and industries, and discussing the state of society with a highly diverse mix of professionals and lay people. The reaction I see coming is a segue into an Era of Responsibility.

Those organizations which take the initiative to help solve the problems of society, including the environment, will be the ones rewarded with loyal customers.

Those organizations which take immediate, clear, and transparent responsibility for fixing any problems they cause – including immediate acknowledgement of their errors, sincere apologies for their mistakes, rapid action to fix their messes, and the required investment to prevent a repeat of the problem – will be forgiven by customers and go unpunished.

Those which do not will quickly lose customers, loyalty, sales, and profits as their misdeeds will promptly and swiftly be broadcast through all social media and Internet channels.

For the past two decades, it seems that fear, greed, and egos have been the most established drivers of successful businesses and their leaders. The backlash to this will be consumers demanding ethics, morality, fairness, mutual respect, and social contribution in their dealings with business and government entities.

This conclusion is supported by the findings of the third annual Edelman goodpurpose™ Consumer Study of 6,000 people in 10 countries, which showed that an increasing number of people are spending on brands that have a social purpose, despite the prolonged stagnant or slow growth in global economies.

In this study, 57% of respondents globally said a company or brand has earned their business because it has been doing its part to support good causes. Most interestingly, the countries reporting the highest level of such consumer support were China (85%) and India (84%). Two-thirds (67%) globally also reported they would switch brands if another brand of similar quality supported a good cause, which means that a corporation's or brand's identification with supporting social causes would be a key differentiator between brands with similar features and attributes.

As Mitch Markson, Edelman's Chief Executive Officer, stated when these survey results were released, "People are demanding social purpose, and brands are recognizing it as an area where they can differentiate themselves, not only to meet government compliance requirements, but also to build brand equity."

In a sign of hope for the world that our children will inherit, the vast majority (87%) of respondents to this survey globally agreed it was their duty to contribute to a better society and environment and 82% feel they can personally make a difference. But here is the number most important to marketers: 83% are willing to change their own consumption habits to help make tomorrow's world a better place.

The Edelman study also revealed that 70% of consumers felt their ability to make monetary financial contributions to community causes had been limited or reduced by the global recession; many had instead given more time in support of good causes because they had not been able to contribute as much financially as in the past.

I draw another conclusion from these results. It appears to me that consumers are also attempting to make indirect financial contributions to the charities and causes they support, through the brands and products they purchase. Someone who has not been able to make their regular donation to the annual Breast Cancer fund drive (for instance), is highly likely to start purchasing products that support Breast Cancer research and which are adorned with the Pink Ribbon support label on the product packaging.

This way they can still feel like they are making some financial contribution to their preferred causes, even when their current financial situation has prevented them from their more generous and direct contributions. The challenge for marketers is how to maintain loyalty from these new purchasers, even when they revert to their generous charitable contributions once the economy rebounds and their personal situations improve.

One way to do so is to be authentic in how your organization approaches its social contributions. While the Edelman survey clearly reveals that social purpose has become increasingly important to a brand's success, the report findings also state, "a brand's purpose must be authentic and true to the core values of the brand itself and brands must look beyond traditional corporate social responsibility programs in which they simply donate money to a good cause."

As the survey notes, 66% of the respondents in these 10 countries no longer believe it is good enough for corporations and brands to merely give money away to charitable causes. The belief now is that, to be authentic, corporations and brands must truly integrate good causes into their day-to-day business activities, as well as into their internal processes and procedures.

This takes the concept of Engagement Marketing to an entirely new level.

Authenticity and trust will be two of the key cornerstones for corporate reputations in this Era of Responsibility. This will come not only from your policies and public pronouncements, but from the actions and beliefs of your employees.

I highly commend to you a four-minute video on YouTube featuring Corporate Philosopher Roger Steare, Professor of Ethics at London's Cass Business School, in which he says, "Money is simply a promissory trust. When we break promises and we break trust, we destroy money, which is what we have seen in the past two years on a global scale."

The Era of Responsibility is not a fad that will pass and be quickly forgotten once economies return to substantial growth levels.

It is a trend that is going to impact elections, market share, social institutions, and the composition of the various stock market indices around the world. Like most trends, those who get in front at the beginning will be the ones who remain ahead as the tide carries others along.

I read with great interest a few years ago that La Trobe University's Graduate School of Management will present Australia's first Master's Degree wholly focused on corporate responsibility – the Masters of Corporate Responsibility. I, for one, cannot wait for the day when MCR degrees out number MBA degrees.

Hopefully this initiative by La Trobe University will catch on like wild fire at universities across the world. Until then, enter the Era of Responsibility with due caution and with the principles of morality, humanity, and doing the right thing in business as espoused by Corporate Philosopher Roger Steare in the above video clip and in his book *Ethicability*.

And remember, authenticity is required when engaging customers and stakeholders in the Era of Responsibility.

More important, every organization has a responsibility to ensure that our children inherit a better world.

**KEY POINT**: authenticity is required when engaging customers and stakeholders in the Era of Responsibility.

**TAKING ACTION**: what are the core beliefs concerning responsibility within your organization?

What lessons are there for your organization from the way Toyota and BP have handled / mishandled their recent responsibility challenges?

What social purposes matter most to your customers? How can your organization authentically support these causes?

What are the three most important things your organization should be doing to ensure our children inherit a better world?

Contact us today for a free in-depth discussion on how we can help you assess your organization's brand strengths and authentically enter the Era of Responsibility.

**#225**

# Customer Retention Marketing

The world in which marketing takes place continues to change and evolve at a rapid pace.

Reduced trade barriers, extensive deregulation across numerous industries, an increasingly globalized economy, customers who are more aware of the choices available to them, and changing customer values are all combining to ignite a dramatic increase in the competition between products, brands, services, companies and, indeed, even countries.

Additionally, customers themselves are changing, particularly in terms of customer needs and their motivations for making purchase decisions. The natural loyalty of customers is quickly becoming a thing of the past, not just because customers have become more fickle, but also because the large majority of organizations do not exhibit the tendencies and criteria that deserve customer loyalty.

Simply put, customers today give their business, and more important their repeat business, to the organizations that do the best job of understanding and responding to their individual needs, wants, desires, likes, and dislikes.

In this highly competitive marketing environment, organizations need to move from a transaction focus and product line focus to a *customer focus*.

Highly successful firms of the future will take this a step further, by developing techniques to continuously learn from interactions with customers and by implementing procedures that enable them to deepen relationships by properly responding to the insights gained from these interactions.

One of the purposes of our marketing philosophy ***Customer Retention: The Art of Keeping Good Customers***™ is to help organizational leaders move beyond the primeval and self-centered goals of Customer Relationship Management to a business philosophy that is more likely to result in the retention of the customer relationships critical to continued and sustainable success.

In doing so, the objectives of the current CRM focus (attempting to manage customer relationships), will evolve into ones more likely to secure long-term customer relationships and result in customer retention:

1) Build, sustain, and cultivate long-term, valuable relationships with customers who are likely to provide beneficial influence over several years.

2) Engage in two-way, bi-mutual communications at every point of contact and interaction in order to learn more about the individual needs, wants,

desires, likes, and dislikes of customers and to strengthen the relationships *between* the organization and its core loyal customer base.

3) Maximize these relationships by providing on-going benefits to your customers and being rewarded with the attitude of customer satisfaction **turning into the behavior of customer loyalty through repeat purchases.**

One of the biggest challenges facing businesses today is that products and services are becoming increasingly commoditized. As a result, one of the only remaining ways to distinguish your products and services is in the relationships you have with your customers.

In the past, being customer-oriented has meant operating in order to meet the needs of the *typical customer*.

Businesses today cannot afford to focus on the average customer. Your future growth, and future profitability, comes from satisfying the needs of your most valuable customers.

To treat your most valuable customers *not as average customers*, but as **your most valued customers**, requires that they be treated as individuals – with individual needs, wants, desires, likes, and dislikes.

This is the true essence behind our marketing philosophy *Customer Retention: The Art of Keeping Good Customers.*

**KEY POINT:** customers today give their business, and more important their **repeat business**, to the organizations that do the best job of understanding and responding to their individual needs, wants, desires, likes, and dislikes.

**TAKING ACTION:** does your organization *respect* the needs, wants, desires, likes, and dislikes of your customers and prospects, or do you see your customers only in terms of the transactions they make with you?

Does your organization try to *understand* the unique needs, wants, desires, likes, and dislikes of your customers and prospects? Or does your organization consider customization requests and flexible requirements to be troublesome and bothersome?

Do you **appreciate** that customers seek convenience and do you have the processes in place that enhance convenience to your customers?

Are you in the business of *solving* problems for your customers, or merely in the business of making products and creating services, while hoping that someone will purchase these?

**#230**

# 4 Ps of Customer Retention (Part One)

It has been almost 50 years since marketing professor (and subsequent guru) Dr. Philip Kotler coined the Four Ps of marketing –– product, price, place, and promotion.

While still very valid today, Kotler's original Four Ps do not have as much application to customer retention as they do to customer acquisition.

A more appropriate set of Four Ps for the area of customer retention would be:

People

Policies

Processes/Procedures

Prevention

Like Kotler's original Four Ps, these four are also inward looking. But, unlike the traditional Four Ps learned in every basic marketing course, the Four Ps of Customer Retention are designed to be applied to current customers already captured through the time-honored marketing mix.

We will cover the first two (People and Policies) this week and the other two next week.

**People** — staff must be motivated, trained and allowed to be customer focused. TLC – think like customers – should be the standard operating procedure.

Staff should have a willingness to listen to customer concerns and to ask questions that uncover the full nature of these concerns. Care for the customer is accentuated by a consistent display of service ethics.

The internal culture of the organization should maximize the willingness of all staff to work well with co-workers and to foster a desire to learn jobs outside their immediate areas of responsibility. Most important, you want staff that constantly exhibit high energy and enthusiasm *for your customers.*

**Goal: do not let your people drive your customers away!**

**Policies** — your policies must be flexible, expandable, and customizable. I highly recommend eliminating the phrase ***it's our policy*** from your organization's vocabulary. Train and empower your staff, particularly frontline customer-facing staff, in interpreting and applying corporate policies as *guidelines* on how to conduct business and engage with customers.

Policies that concern corporate ethics, safety, or areas that could have *major* impact on profitability should certainly be followed to the letter. However, policies that have to do with internal procedures and processes, and which have a direct impact on your organization's ability to meet *individual* customer needs, should be used as guidelines to help employees deal with specific customer situations.

**Goal: do not let your policies anger your customers!**

In my mind, customer retention is *the art of keeping good customers.*™

This art is best applied through a concentrated focus on the Four P's of Customer Retention.

We will cover the other two (Processes/Procedures and Prevention) in next week's *Monday Morning Marketing Memo.*

In the interim, see our 7 Cs of Customer Retention Checklist in the Tool Section at the back of this book for more ideas on how to keep good customers.

**KEY POINTS:** 1) do not let your people drive your customers away, and 2) do not let your policies anger your customers.

**TAKING ACTION:** what can you do to make your products and services *real for customers?* To begin with, train your staff to Think Like Customers. If your staff can not understand a customer's need, want, desire, like, or dislike, then they will have a more difficult time resolving a customer's complaint.

Review your policies and procedures. When were these written? Do they still make sense or are they more a reflection of "that's the way we have always done things"? Which polices and procedures may be too rigid for today's customers?

# 4 Ps of Customer Retention (Part Two)

As we mentioned last week, it has been approximately 50 years since marketing professor (and subsequent guru) Dr. Philip Kotler coined the Four Ps of marketing —- product, price, place, and promotion.

While still very valid today, Kotler's original Four Ps do not have as much application to customer retention as they do to customer acquisition.

A more appropriate set of Four Ps for the area of customer retention would be:

People

Policies

Processes/Procedures

Prevention

In last week's Monday Morning Marketing Memo we covered the first two (People and Policies). We will now give you an overview of the importance of Processes/Procedures and Prevention on customer retention.

**Processes/Procedures** — your processes and procedures need to be made as simplistic and straight-forward as possible, in order to provide greater convenience, speed, and ease of access to your products and services for customers.

Sign-offs and authorization procedures should be more streamlined for existing customers than for prospects and new customers. When in doubt, reduce odious procedures and simplify processes for existing customers by granting them higher levels of trust.

For instance, why must a hotel require a credit card imprint at check-in from a guest who has stayed in that hotel numerous times before? After all, a returning guest with a multiple stay record is unlikely to abscond without paying his or her room bill.

**Goal: do not let your procedures and processes inconvenience your customers!**

**Prevention** — one of my deep-seated marketing beliefs is preventing customer complaints is better than resolving them. In my second job, while still in high school, the owner of the business taught me his 7 Ps of Business Success (please excuse the language): proper prior planning prevents piss-poor performance.

Despite his inelegant language, his point was well taken. No wonder he is still in business today, some 40 years later!

To keep good customers, your organization needs to commit to quality (as defined by your customers) from the top down and the bottom up. Eliminate errors and you eradicate many of the key reasons customers have for leaving.

**Goal: do not let mistakes cause your customers to leave!**

Like Kotler's original Four P's, the Four Ps of Customer Retention are all focused inward on your organization. But, unlike the traditional Four Ps learned in every basic marketing course, the Four Ps of Customer Retention are designed to be applied to current customers already captured through the time-honored marketing mix.

In my mind, customer retention *is the art of keeping good customers*. This art is best applied through a concentrated emphasis on the Four Ps of Customer Retention — People, Policies, Processes/Procedures, and Prevention — combined with the 7 Cs of Customer Retention.

Awaken these 4 Ps and 7 Cs in your organization, and watch your customer retention levels ascend to heights previously only dreamed.

**KEY POINTS**: 1) do not let your procedures and processes inconvenience your customers, and 2) do not let mistakes cause your customers to leave.

**TAKING ACTION**: ask yourself (or better yet, ask your customers) is your organization easy to do business with? What rules, procedures, and processes do you have that makes it hard for your customers to do business with you?

How could you make it easier for customers to do business with you? What changes could you make in the areas of convenience, order placement, product or service customization, delivery, or other terms and conditions that would make it easier for customers to do business with you?

Contact me today for an in-depth discussion on how I can help you design and implement a strategic customer retention program for your business. We have helped organizations large and small reduce customer attrition and keep good customers.

# Tools

We are pleased to share with you some of the marketing tools and checklists provided to our clients and *Monday Morning Marketing Memo* readers over the years:

7 Cs of Customer Retention Checklist

Five Dimensions of Service Quality Excellence

Six Steps to SEO Success

8 Common SEO Mistakes

17 Costly Marketing Mistakes

# 7 Cs of Customer Retention Checklist

## 1. *Caring Attitude*

*Projecting a caring attitude through:*

- tone of voice

- use of pleasantries (please, thank you)

- smile projection

- empathy

- language (minimal use of industry jargon)

- taking ownership

- going the "extra mile" on behalf of customer

## 2. *Customized Practices*

*Definition of customizing:*

- Treating customers as individuals at all points of interaction.

- Making exceptions to policies / procedures to meet individual customer needs, wants, desires, likes, and dislikes.

- Empowering customer contact personnel.

- Using the customer's name in conversation.

- Ensuring the customer knows the contact person's name.

- Specific empowerment:

  - approval limits
  - policy waiver limits
  - waiver of fees/charges
  - temporary credit line increases

### 3. *Competent Customer Contact Personnel*

*Projecting knowledge and confidence through:*

- Knowledge of organization's products.

- Knowledge of organization's services.

- Knowledge of organization's policies and procedures.

- Knowledge of inter-company and inter-departmental processes.

- Availability of customer's account information to all staff.

- Availability of customer's purchase history to all staff.

4. *Call/Visit Once*

*Eliminating the need for customers to repeat information:*

- Add information to statements / invoices to eliminate calls.

- Put mailing address on payment voucher section of invoices/statements.

- Determine most convenient way *for the customer* for you to correspond with the customer (letter, fax, form letter, email).

- Create internal infrastructure so customer always talks / meets with same customer contact person.

- Track how often each customer contact person handles an entire call and resolves problems without having to refer to others or pass off to others.

- Implement internal infrastructure and policies on when it is okay to transfer customer to another staff (e.g. under what circumstances, how this should be handled, what is an acceptable number of times to be transferred?).

- Having a process to transfer customer's situation, details, and desired outcome when transferring customer to another staff.

- How / when can customer talk to a supervisor or a manager if needed on the same call?

- Call once does not necessarily mean speaking with only one person; it means the issue gets resolved within that call *or the organization calls the customer back* until the issue is resolved.

- Allow customer contact person to call customer back (but *must* be within promised timeframe and at a time convenient to the customer).

## 5. *Convenient Access*

*Access to your organization should be convenient to the customer when it is most convenient for them:*

- How can 24/7 service be provided?

- How can 24/7 access be efficiently provided?

- What transactions can be self-service?

- How do customers define access? Operating hours? Type of access?

♦ How can you provide relevant information that eliminates the need for customers to contact your organization?

## 6. *Compressed Cycle Times*

*In today's world, everything must be done faster:*

♦ Eliminate busy signals.

♦ Reduce call waiting times and decrease how often customers are put "on hold."

♦ Track resolution times for specific problems.

♦ Know what customers' time expectations for resolution are.

♦ Speed up correspondence response times to customers, especially for email and website generated correspondence.

♦ What services should be handled by phone? Via the Internet? In person?

♦ How do anticipated time frames differ for different issues?

## 7. *Committed Follow Through*

*Commitment is both an individual act and an organizational promise:*

♦ Timeliness of follow through.

♦ Format for follow through (letter, phone call, email, fax, other).

♦ How can customer contact person make customers confident that action will be taken and that it will be taken in a timely manner?

♦ Customer contact personnel should have the attitude "if I touch it, it's mine to resolve or to *ensure* that it is resolved by someone else."

# Five Dimensions of Service Quality Excellence

Excellent customer service and service quality excellence are defined by customer satisfaction, resulting in a strategic advantage with a direct impact on repeat business, customer recommendations to others, market share, revenue, and profit.

Customer satisfaction is created by delivering upon the Five Dimensions of Service Quality that are the most important to customers:

**Customization** — this can be accomplished in terms of tonality, or adopting the right kind of concerned, interested, friendly tone of voice. Even by using the customer's correct name, your Customer Contact Personnel (CCP) can create an immediate, positive impression that the customer is being treated as an individual. Customization can also be created through the use of technology. By being supplied with the right customer information, the CCP can customize transactions to the meet the customer's individual requirements.

**Comprehension** — requires listening skills, patience, and empathy. It also requires technology that facilitates teamwork throughout the organization, especially between front office and back office staffs, for the benefit of the customer. This will enable successful problem solving (and problem prevention), which will reduce customer attrition.

**Convenience** — is one of the major reason people buy services and products. The easier the access to their accounts, and to customer service delivery, the more likely current customers will remain and new customers will trial your product and service offers.

**Compression** — means shortening the time it takes for customers to transact with or to learn about an organization's products. Specific areas of compression might be: 1) answering the phone by the third ring, 2) reducing the amount of time customers spend on hold, and 3) solving the customer's problems through the right combination of technology and CCP empowerment.

**Consistency** — simply means that customers can expect, and will receive, the same level of customer service experience every time they call, visit, or interact with the organization. Standards have to be maintained at all points of customer contact, with no allowance for any occasional letdowns.

# Six Steps to SEO Success

Here are six key elements of *basic* Search Engine Optimization that need to be performed (and maintained) on any website:

1. Identifying page title, page descriptions and page keywords -- these are the critical elements that the search engines look for when they review a site and log the details of that site. It is this information that is then presented to Internet users in the search results they see.

2. Re-writing and editing the copy on *each page* of the website for SEO relevancy and sufficient use of keywords and key search phrases.

3. Having internal links between pages of the website using anchor text.

4. Getting listed with online directories and search engines (an important, but tedious process that takes time, some special knowledge, and the right set of software tools).

5. Creating other critical inbound links from websites with authority and relevance to your products and services, including through the use of Social Media Marketing channels (Facebook, Google+, Twitter, YouTube, Instagram, etc.)

6. Keeping website content fresh and updated.

As we mentioned last week, since **70% of all "clicks" on Internet searches are for the organic results**, and only 30% are on the paid advertising results, the importance of Search Engine Optimization cannot be overstated.

Additionally when it comes to website writing, a good website writer has to have strong copywriting skills with a marketing background, **a clear understanding of how prospective customers and repeat visitors will interact with a client's website**, and comprehensive knowledge of how Google and the other search engines use spiders to crawl and rank website pages.

Point Six above on keeping content fresh and updated is now mandatory. Google has changed in recent months and now gives higher rankings to website pages that have recently been updated and changed. Website pages that are static and unchanged for long periods of time (i.e. more than a couple of months) will now suffer in the Google search engine results.

# 8 Common SEO Mistakes

Your website should enhance the credibility and reputation of your business, generated sales leads and attract prospective customers, or both.

For your website to be an effective sales and marketing tool, you need to drive traffic to it. And that's where Search Engine Optimization (SEO) comes in. Unfortunately, this is also where a lot of small business owners and entrepreneurs fall down, most due to a lack of knowledge on how to implement a SEO strategy.

Here are the eight most common SEO mistakes I see small businesses, industry associations and entrepreneurs making:

1. **Writing for Google** -- websites need to be written for their human readers, with the search engines kept in mind but not as the main focus of the copywriting.

There is an art to writing a good website that is highly readable and informative, while simultaneously being highly functional to search engines. Great website copywriting also eliminates the mistakes of repetitious keywords and a lack of internal links (see below). Also, Google now penalizes sites that have spelling errors, another good reason to ensure you use a professional writer for your site.

2. **Wrong or no header information** -- technically called H1 and H2 headers, these need to incorporate key search phrases, not your company name or product brands. These should be written with search phrases in mind, and not advertising taglines or marketing slogans (unless you believe prospects or customers are likely to search on your advertising taglines and marketing slogans).

3. **Repetitious keywords** -- while it is important to include all your important keywords and key search phrases within your website, it is not necessary to do so on each and every page. This is especially true if your URL or company name already includes an important search phrase. For instance, if you are "ABC Public Relations" then you do not need to use "public relations" on every page. Instead, highlight other services you might provide, such as government relations, press relations, media relations and media training. It is best to use a wide range of keywords and key search phrases throughout your website. Remember, it is not important to drive traffic only to your home page. Drive traffic to the other key pages of your website as well.

4. **Keyword stuffing** -- even worse than repetitious keyword usage is keyword stuffing, for Google actually

penalizes websites for this. Keyword stuffing is basically any annoying repeating of the same keyword or search phrase over and over again on the same page. For instance: cheap airfares to Hong Kong, cheap airfares to Phuket, cheap airfares to Bangkok, cheap airfares to Gold Coast, etc. Trying to win better search results by stuffing a page with too many "cheap airfare" phrases will no longer fool Google.

5. **Competing with own pages** -- this is probably the most common error for those who actually have some SEO in place. Repeating the same header tag and page descriptions across numerous pages simply confuses Google, and hence it does not know how to properly evaluate and rank such pages. As a result, your own pages end up fighting with each other for Google's attention. Each page should have its own and unique header tag and page descriptions should be modified,

even if slightly, so that each can attract different search phrases and keywords.

6. **Not using ALT Text for images** -- Google cannot read an image, so each image you use should have ALT Text that reflects an important keyword or key search phrase.

7. **Trying to trick Google** -- the last few years have seen a constant battle between people trying to trick the search engines, with Google and others fighting back by changing their algorithms. Using hidden text or keywords not relevant to your site will no longer trick Google. And most likely anything else someone suggests you do, other than having relevant text, strong header tags, and concise page descriptions, will not trick Google for long. If someone put these in place for you previously, they need to be removed quickly.

8. **Lack of links** -- you still need *relevant* inbound links, but don't go out and try to buy hundreds of links from so-called link farms. This old trick no longer works either and, in fact, may actually hurt your search results. Also, many websites do not use anchor text for internal links, or have a lack of internal links. Both are costly errors in terms of SEO. And by the way, all "click here" instructions in body text are useless in terms of SEO.

It doesn't matter how big your business is, or in which industry your business is in. It doesn't matter where you are, or where your customers are. A proper SEO program will make a major difference in the returns you gain from your website.

SEO prominence is an important winning marketing strategy, giving a smart business a competitive edge in the all-important search results that prospective buyers and customers see when conducting online searches for products,

services and solutions to their needs.

# 17 Costly Marketing Mistakes

I once heard a speaker describe those who engage in marketing as *"feeling happy like a dog with its head outside the car window, ears flapping, eyes glazed, and no idea of where he's going."*

Now I will be the first to admit that marketing is not rocket science. But I will also be the first to tell you that marketing is an art that uses some scientific disciplines (such as market research and statistical analysis) and not a science in and of itself. Not understanding the art of marketing is often the difference between failure and success.

Over the years I have coached and worked with numerous business owners and entrepreneurs on how to market their businesses better. In doing so, I have compiled a list of 17 of the most common and costly marketing mistakes made by business owners, company executives, and professional service providers.

Avoiding these mistakes will not only help you know where your business is going, it will also enable you to attract the right set of core customers; thus helping to ensure the long-term sustainable growth of your business.

Here's my list of 17 Costly Marketing Mistakes:

**1. Messages do not speak to your prospects** – customers have problems for which they seek solutions. Your marketing messages need to be concise and clear about what you can do *for them* and what benefits they will gain from doing business with you. If your messages are *all about you,* then it is hard for prospects to understand the WIIFT (what's in it for them).

**2. Messages do not speak *with* your customers** – successful marketing is a two-way dialogue with your customers, not a one-way barrage of messages from you to them. Your marketing should aim to solicit feedback and input from customers, particularly about other problems they currently have or are likely to face in the future. By understanding and anticipating customer needs you can develop new products and services, or form new partnerships, that provide the solutions your customers will purchase.

**3. Marketing materials are not professional looking** – your marketing materials need to project your professionalism. Photocopied flyers and brochures are for amateurs. It is simple to design and print quality flyers, information sheets, and promotional materials using basic software such as Microsoft Publisher. If you do not have the time to do this yourself, hire a high school or college student. Students today are well versed in computer graphics and the cost of printing a few hundred flyers in color is next to nothing.

**4. Advertising in the wrong media** – find out which media your customers are using and put your presence there. Where do your customers turn for information? That's where your advertisements should be. Not in the publications or media that you enjoy.

**5. Promoting features over benefits** – customers do not buy services, they buy solutions. Tell them what you can do for them and what benefits they will gain. A feature is your 10-year career. A benefit is that you will relieve the pain in my back. A better benefit is that you'll teach me how to prevent or minimize back pain in the future.

**6. Assuming your audience understands what you offer** – your customers are not likely to understand the intricacies of one treatment over another. They seek advice from you and the practitioner who does a better job of explaining each treatment and the options available is the one most likely to have repeat customers.

**7. Communicating too many messages** – you have a lot to communicate about your services. However, too many scattered messages cause confusion. Don't try to tell everything in each brochure or advertisement. Focus on one or two key points each time and then point your prospects and customers to a place where they can get more information (like your website).

**8. Failure to cover rational and emotional buying criteria** – customers use both rational and emotional criteria when making any critical purchase decision. Your messages need to appeal to both these aspects, and this is particularly true when they are in your clinic seeking treatment.

**9. A business that is not properly positioned –** there's a huge difference between a Physiotherapy Wellness Centre and a Physiotherapy Clinic. I am sure in your mind's eye your own business is different than the other competitors in your market. Understanding this difference and being able to communicate it is at the heart of positioning. How you position your business will have a direct impact on the types of customers you attract.

**10. Offering non-differentiated services —** if you offer the exact same services as your competitors, with similar operating hours, then the only thing you can compete on is price. There is no such thing as a commodity practice, only practices and businesses that are marketed like commodities. The key to growing any business is having the ability to differentiate your products and services from competitive offerings. Also, offering differentiated services often enables a business to increase margins or create additional revenue streams outside consulting fees.

**11. Failure to continually market the business —** business owners often make two major mistakes when it comes to marketing: a) reducing marketing expenditures during soft economic times, and b) failing to invest in marketing when business is good. Marketing is not a tool that can be turned on and off like a tap. A sustained marketing effort is needed in both good and bad times.

**12. Not looking for new channels of business –** there are numerous ways to grow a practice without increasing the number of therapists and the number of treatment rooms you have. Quite frankly, there is a larger market for helping customers prevent injuries than there is for treating injuries and problems. People pay for gym instructors, nutritionists, holistic therapies, spa treatments, and a wide variety of other services in order to improve their health. Why aren't more of them also paying you for similar advice and services?

**13. Not collecting and capturing information on your customers** – your customer base is one of the most strategic assets in your business, yet very few business owners understand how to leverage this asset. Your customers often have rich and exciting lives that you could tap into, if only you knew more about them. This impacts not only your ability to create new products and services for them, but also your ability to leverage customers for referral business.

**14. Not using satisfied customers for referrals** – a great number of your new clients come to you as referrals from friends and family, yet very few small businesses take a structured approach to using satisfied customers as a channel for new business. Many professionals are reluctant to ask for referrals or even to provide an easy method for customers to recommend them. That's a shame as there are many subtle and soft approaches that work equally as well as bluntly asking customers to give referrals. But like most other marketing tactics, this requires a structured approach.

**15. Not understanding why customers leave –** very few businesses survey lost customers to find out why they have taken their business somewhere else. This is a major mistake. Surveying lost customers can identify problems that you are unaware of, as well as new services offered by others that are taking your clientele away. It is best to use an outside resource to survey lost customers and it is a practice that should be conducted at least annually.

**16. Putting your operational needs before those of your customers** – there are a wide range of choices and options available to customers today. One of the key things customers value is flexibility, and if your operational procedures cannot provide the flexibility to meet changing customer needs, then their business will go elsewhere. Remember, customers are the reason you are in business, and hence your policies and procedures should be designed with customer needs in mind, not just the needs of your staff.

**17. Not having a Web presence** – the Internet has become the number one place where people seek out information, even for local providers and services. Not having your own website results in lost business and a missed opportunity to provide in-depth information about your products and services on a 24/7 basis. Also, an electronic newsletter is an inexpensive way to keep your name in front of your customers and prospects on a regular basis, while also enabling the effects of viral marketing to take place when your readers pass on your newsletter to friends and family.

My personal marketing philosophy is quite simple: *if it touches the customer, it's a marketing issue.*™

Everything you and your colleagues do touches your customers, in more ways than one. This includes the way you communicate with customers and the methods you use in trying to attract new customers.

Marketing is one of the strategic propellers of any successful business. You cannot have a successful business without engaging in successful marketing. Likewise, engaging in successful marketing increases the odds of creating a successful and sustainable business.

The mistakes listed above are tactical in nature. The most common strategic marketing mistake made by many small (and large) businesses is putting a greater focus on attracting new customers than in retaining current good customers.

There are only three ways to grow any business:

- Increase the number of customers.

- Persuade your current customers to buy more (larger volumes).

- Encourage your current customers to buy more often (from you).

Two of the three ways to grow a business, therefore, are reliant on building relationships and increased purchases from existing customers. And, quite frankly, in terms of increasing the number of total customers, this is often dependent on how you treat your current customers since a large percentage of new customers will come through referrals by existing customers.

In today's world, with so many choices and options available to customers, if you do not take care of your customers, someone else will. The best way to take care of your customers is to create true value for them. This is best done by ensuring everyone in your organization has a passion for customers and by developing a better understanding of customers and their unique needs.

You will probably have noticed that I use the word "customers" throughout this article. While you may think of your clientele as "patients," I would encourage you to also start thinking of them as *customers*. For that's what they truly are – customers who are exercising their decisions on what to buy and with which organization they will do business.

Each of you knows how you like to be treated as a customer when you are the ones buying a product or service. When you think of your patients as customers, your mindset will change and you will have a better inkling on how your customers want to be treated.

After all, the great businesses of tomorrow will be grown exactly the way great businesses have always been built – by doing marvelous things that meet the needs, wants, and desires of customers.

Which is why one of my key pieces of advice to my own customers is always **don't have a commitment to customer service – have a commitment to your customers.**

When you do this, not only will your eyes be glazed and your ears flapping, you'll also know where you are headed –– as the owner of a sustainable and growing business.

# About the Author

**Steven Howard**
**Author, Blogger, Marketing and Branding**
**Strategist**

Steven Howard is a leading marketing strategist, positioning specialist, consultant, and author whose 38-year marketing and sales career in Asia, Australia, and the USA has covered a wide variety of fields, ranging from consumer electronics to publishing and from a national airline to personal financial products.

Founder of **Howard Marketing Services**, he has consulted to companies in the financial services, education, industrial products, consumer products, restaurants, petroleum, publishing, and hospitality fields. In 2014 he was named to a list of the Global Top 100 SEO Copywriters.

He is the author of nine other books:

*Corporate Image Management: A Marketing Discipline*

*Powerful Marketing Minutes: 50 Ways to Develop Market Leadership*

*MORE Powerful Marketing Minutes: 50 New Ways to Develop Market Leadership*

*Asian Words of Wisdom*

*Asian Words of Knowledge*

*Essential Asian Words of Wisdom*

*Pillars of Growth: Strategies for Leading Sustainable Growth* (co-author with three others)

*Motivation Plus Marketing Equals Money* (co-author with four others)

*Marketing Words of Wisdom*

He also writes the *Monday Morning Marketing Memo Blog*, *The Steven Howard Marketing Blog*, as well as the *Keeping Good Customers Blog*.

## Contact Details
Email: steven@howard-marketing.com

Twitter: @stevenbhoward

LinkedIn: www.linkedin.com/in/stevenbhoward

Facebook: facebook.com/MondayMorningMarketingMemo

Website: www.howard-marketing.com

Blog: www.TheMondayMorningMarketingMemo.com

www.ingramcontent.com/pod-product-compliance
Lightning Source LLC
Chambersburg PA
CBHW031417220326
41520CB00059B/6771